Match of My Life

IPSWICH TOWN

KNOW THE SCORE BOOKS SPORTS PUBLICATIONS

CULT HEROES	Author	ISBN
ABERDEEN	Paul Smith	978-1-84818-104-5
CARLISLE UNITED	Mark Harrison	978-1-905449-09-7
CELTIC	David Potter	978-1-905449-08-8
CHELSEA	Leo Moynihan	1-905449-00-3
MANCHESTER CITY	David Clayton	978-1-905449-05-7
NEWCASTLE	Dylan Younger	1-905449-03-8
NOTTINGHAM FOREST	David McVay	978-1-905449-06-4
RANGERS	Paul Smith	978-1-905449-07-1
SOUTHAMPTON	Jeremy Wilson	1-905449-01-1
WEST BROM	Simon Wright	1-905449-02-X

MATCH OF MY LIFE	Editor	ISBN
BRIGHTON	Paul Camillin	978-1-84818-000-0
DERBY COUNTY	Nick Johnson	978-1-905449-68-2
ENGLAND WORLD CUP	Massarella & Moynihan	1-905449-52-6
EUROPEAN CUP FINALS	Ben Lyttleton	1-905449-57-7
FA CUP FINALS 1953-1969	David Saffer	978-1-905449-53-8
FULHAM	Michael Heatley	1-905449-51-8
IPSWICH TOWN	Mel Henderson	978-1-84818-001-7
LEEDS	David Saffer	1-905449-54-2
LIVERPOOL	Leo Moynihan	1-905449-50-X
MANCHESTER UNITED	Ivan Ponting	978-1-905449-59-0
SHEFFIELD UNITED	Nick Johnson	1-905449-62-3
STOKE CITY	Simon Lowe	978-1-905449-55-2
SUNDERLAND	Rob Mason	1-905449-60-7
SPURS	Allen & Massarella	978-1-905449-58-3
WOLVES	Simon Lowe	1-905449-56-9

GENERAL FOOTBALL	Author	ISBN
2006 WORLD CUP DIARY	Harry Harris	1-905449-90-9
BEHIND THE BACK PAGE	Christopher Davies	978-1-84818-506-7
BOOK OF FOOTBALL OBITUARIES	Ivan Ponting	978-1-905449-82-2
BURKSEY	Peter Morfoot	1-905449-49-6
FORGIVE US OUR PRESS PASSES	Football Writers' Association	978-1-84818-507-4
HOLD THE BACK PAGE	Harry Harris	1-905449-91-7
JUST ONE OF SEVEN	Denis Smith	978-1-84818-504-3

MAN & BABE	Wilf McGuinness	978-1-84818-503-6
MANCHESTER UNITED: PLAYER BY PLAYER		
	Ivan Ponting	978-1-84818-500-1
MY PREMIERSHIP DIARY	Marcus Hahnemann	978-1-905449-33-0
OUTCASTS	Steve Menary	978-1-905449-31-6
The Lands That FIFA Forgot		
PALLY: My Story	Gary Pallister	978-1-84818-500-5
PARISH TO PLANET	Eric Midwinter	978-1-905449-30-9
A History of Football		
PLEASE MAY I HAVE MY FOOTBALL BACK?		
	Eric Alexander	978-1-84818-508-1
TACKLES LIKE A FERRET	Paul Parker	1-905449-47-X
(England Cover)		
TACKLES LIKE A FERRET	Paul Parker	1-905449-46-1
(Manchester United Cover)		
TOTTENHAM HOTSPUR: PLAYER BY PLAYER		
	Ivan Ponting	978-1-84818-501-
THE DOOG	Harrison & Gordos	978-1-84818-502-9
THE RVALS GAME	Douglas Beattie	978-1-905449-79-8

RUGBY LEAGUE	Author	ISBN
MOML LEEDS RHINOS	Caplan & Saffer	978-1-905449-69-9
MOML WIGAN WARRIORS	David Kuzio	978-1-905449-66-8

CRICKET	Author	ISBN
ASHES TO DUST	Graham Cookson	978-1-905449-19-4
CRASH! BANG! WALLOP!	Martyn Hindley	978-1-905449-88-0
GROVEL!	David Tossell	978-1-905449-43-9
MOML: THE ASHES	Pilger & Wightman	1-905449-63-1
MY TURN TO SPIN	Shaun Udal	978-1-905449-42-2
WASTED?	Paul Smith	978-1-905449-45-3

Match of My Life

IPSWICH TOWN

Editor: Mel Henderson

www.knowthescorebooks.com

First published in the United Kingdom
by Know The Score Books Limited, 2008

Know The Score Books Limited
118 Alcester Road
Studley
Warwickshire
B80 7NT
01527 454482
info@knowthescorebooks.com
www.knowthescorebooks.com

A CIP catalogue record is available for this book from the British Library
ISBN: 978-1-84818-001-7

Jacket design by Graham Hales

Printed and bound in Great Britain by
TJ International Ltd, Padstow, Cornwall

Front cover:

Top: Alf Ramsey was a miracle worker of a manager, first leading Ipswich to the League Championship in 1962 and England to the World Cup four years later.

Middle: Defensive stalwarts Kevin Beattie, left, and Allan Hunter proudly display the FA Cup after the 1-0 win over Arsenal at Wembley in 1978.

Bottom: Wembley again as player turned manager Jim Magilton celebrates after the play-off final win over Barnsley that restored Ipswich to the Premiership in 2000.

Rear cover:

Top left: Scoring against Manchester United is good enough but when it helps your team to a 6-0 win it's all the more memorable. Alan Brazil celebrates Town's triumph in March 1980.

Top right: The Ipswich squad for the 1969/70 season. Back row, left to right, Mick Lambert, Derek Jefferson, Charlie Woods, Ron Wigg, David Best, John O'Rourke, Bobby Bell, Mick McNeil. Front row, Mick Mills, Colin Harper, Peter Morris, Bill Baxter, Tommy Carroll, Ian Collard, Clive Woods. Sitting in front, Steve Stacey and Frank Brogan.

Bottom: Job done, John Wark and Terry Butcher look ahead to the UEFA Cup Final after the latter's goal in Cologne earned Ipswich victory in the second leg of the semi-final.

Editor's Acknowledgements

The most important and heartfelt thanks must go to the players catalogued here, who gave so generously and selflessly of their time. They are an enormous credit to the sport they grace.

It helped, of course, that I have known most of them for many years, but their co-operation is nevertheless much appreciated and I am also extremely grateful for their considerable powers of recall.

Thanks go to Simon Lowe and his staff at Know the Score for their help, assistance and understanding along the way.

Mel Henderson
September 2008

THIS BOOK IS DEDICATED TO THE
LATE JOHN COBBOLD, THE FORMER
IPSWICH TOWN CHAIRMAN WHOSE
UNIQUE PERSONALITY PUT THE
CLUB IN A LEAGUE OF ITS OWN.

Contents

Introduction

It was during my return journey, having met Simon Lowe of Know The Score Books for the very first time to both discuss and agree the project, that I first began formulating in my head a list of those players I would like to feature in this book. Needless to say, given Ipswich Town's rich and eventful history, it soon became an exercise in trying to whittle the number down so as to still represent the club's monumental feat in winning the League Championship at the very first time of asking under Alf Ramsey's astute management, plus the FA Cup and UEFA Cup triumphs masterminded by Bobby Robson, as well as reflecting the club's many other exploits both in this country and abroad that have captured the imagination of supporters over the years.

Given that the club only turned professional in 1936, were admitted to the Football League in 1938 and that the Second World War promptly disrupted football for the next few years, it was not until 1946 that Ipswich properly started out on a remarkable journey that carried them, via successes in the Third Division (South) and Second Division, to the very pinnacle of the domestic scene just 16 years later. As someone undoubtedly privileged to witness so many of the great games and players that illuminated the Robson years, including all 66 of the club's fixtures in the unforgettable 1980/81 campaign, I envy those amongst you who saw the Ramsey fairytale unfold and especially those who witnessed the unbelievable achievement of newly-promoted Town being crowned Champions of England in 1962.

The next best thing, however, was to interview title-winning heroes John Elsworthy, Ted Phillips, Ray Crawford and Larry Carberry, all of whom defied their advancing years by painting near-technicolour pictures of football life at that time, providing an enthralling insight into what will remain forever as one of the most fascinating success stories in the history of the English game. As I write this introduction, another season is under way and no-one anticipates a club from outside the top four of Manchester United, Chelsea, Arsenal and Liverpool being able to finish on top of the Premiership, its predictability about as far removed from what occurred all those years ago when Ramsey's team, assembled at minimal cost and featuring a number of other club's discards, was simply without equal.

While their financial rewards may have been embarrassingly modest, Messrs Elsworthy, Phillips, Crawford and Carberry, as well as their teammates at the time, can be considered rich in as much that they were part of something so infinitely special that it is highly unlikely ever to be repeated. Indeed, no amount of money could possibly compensate for their extraordinary places in the record books and roles in a story that Hollywood moguls, had their soccer knowledge been up to scratch at the time, would have probably rejected as being too far-fetched.

Moving on through the years, and coming right up to date, the reminiscences of the 12 other players featured herein, all of whose accomplishments warrant such recognition, underline the excitement, joy and, in some cases, sheer ecstasy that can be derived from such a simple pleasure as following your favourite football team. Above all else, however, what shone through in each and every one of the conversations was that the ex-players all thoroughly enjoyed their spells in the spotlight and, regardless of the hand that fate has dealt them since, have a wonderful stock of happy memories, many of which will surprise and shock readers, they can call their own.

For my part, while it was an honour to wallow in the company of such a select group, all of whom I should emphasise freely gave of their time, I cannot help but reflect on the bizarre nature of the modern game, offering as it does often obscene riches to participants destined, inevitably, to under-achieve by comparison.

Mel Henderson
September 2008

Foreword

SIR BOBBY ROBSON

Y̶ou cannot possibly devote as large a slice of your life as I did to managing Ipswich Town without having a genuine, lifelong affection for the club.

I spent almost 13 years in the job until I departed to lead my country in 1982, but ever since, regardless of where my work has taken me, I have always made a point of closely following Ipswich's fortunes.

I even recall how, in 1993 during my time as head coach of Sporting Lisbon, Elsie and I managed to find a bar close to our home in which we were able to watch the East Anglian derby win over Norwich. Jason Dozzell, featured in this book because he holds his own special place in the record books, scored twice in that game as I recall.

I felt both privileged and honoured when I was invited to take up the honorary position of President in 2006, and I can honestly say that the depth, and warmth, of my feeling for the club has never diminished.

It is with a great deal of pride that I look back on the many achievements during my tenure, most notably our successes in the FA Cup in 1978 and the UEFA Cup three years later. But while winning two such prestigious competitions will never be forgotten, just as important in my view was how we consistently produced a number of top quality home-grown players. It was with enormous pride that I saw so many of them advance to gain international recognition by their respective countries, as well as featuring prominently when the individual accolades were being handed out.

There was no greater thrill than to see players, some of whom I had first encountered as schoolboys, graduating to establish themselves in the first team, and it gives me enormous pleasure to see that a number of them are featured in this book. Indeed, four of them – Kevin Beattie, Mick Mills, John Wark and Alan Brazil – emerged via the youth team and would all feature in my best-ever Ipswich Town X1, although such was the success of our acquisition of players via the transfer market, in addition to those recruited into our prolific youth system, that I wonder how I could possibly leave anyone out.

Lessons learned at Ipswich – I have never forgotten the 'love the game more than the prize' advice passed on by my former chairman and friend John Cobbold – helped to prepare me for my incredible journey in the game, including a further 22 years as a manager.

Of course, as with life itself, my time in charge at Portman Road had its ups and downs. There were early difficulties and it will always remain a major frustration that we were never quite good enough to win the League Championship, although we did come very close, finishing as runners-up in each of my last two seasons and third on a further three occasions.

Ipswich did, however, land the main domestic honour in 1962 under Alf Ramsey's management and that remains one of the all-time great triumphs in the history of the English game, so it is fitting that four members of that great side – Larry Carberry, John Elsworthy, Ray Crawford and Ted Phillips – are featured herein.

Add the recollections of Roger Osborne, the original local hero after his Wembley winner against Arsenal, and a host of others from a more modern era, and you have a book that will appeal to supporters of all ages who have a special place in their hearts, as I do, for an exceptional club.

Sir Bobby Robson
August 2008

JOHN ELSWORTHY
LEFT-HALF 1949–1965

BORN   26 July 1931, Nantyderry, Monmouthshire
SIGNED   9 May 1949 from amateur
IPSWICH CAREER   435 games, 53 goals
HONOURS   Third Division (South) Championship 1953/54, 1956/57; Second Division Championship 1960/61; First Division Championship 1961/62
LEFT   Retired, 30 June 1965

John holds a unique place in the record books as the only player in Football League history to collect two Third Division (South) title-winning medals before going on to also win both Second Division and First Division medals. An all-round sportsman, he chose football ahead of cricket after he had the opportunity to sign for Glamorgan. He was spotted playing for Newport County's youth team and initially signed on as an amateur. He was paid as a part-timer during a two-year term in the RAF and he went on to spend his entire professional career at Portman Road. A tall, elegant wing-half, he was the brains and the driving force of Alf Ramsey's side crowned Champions of England. After he hung up his boots, he ran a grocery and post office in Ipswich until his retirement. He is now honorary president of the supporters' club and watches all home games. John and Reg Pickett are the only two survivors from the team that took on the Busby Babes.

Manchester United 2 v Ipswich Town 0

FA Cup fourth round
Saturday 25 January 1958

Old Trafford
Attendance 53,550

Ipswich confirm their growing status in English football as they push champions Manchester United all the way in the last game played at Old Trafford before the Munich air disaster

Teams

Matt Busby	**Managers**	Alf Ramsey
Harry Gregg	1	Roy Bailey
Bill Foulkes	2	Basil Acres
Roger Byrne	3	Ken Malcolm
Eddie Colman	4	Reg Pickett
Mark Jones	5	Dai Rees
Duncan Edwards	6	John Elsworthy
Ken Morgans	7	Billy Reed
Bobby Charlton	8	Doug Millward
Tommy Taylor	9	Tom Garneys
Dennis Viollet	10	Derek Rees
Albert Scanlon	11	Jimmy Leadbetter
Charlton 39, 85	Goals	

Referee: Leo Callaghan (Merthyr Tydfil)

WHY, YOU MUST SURELY BE wondering, has someone who played 435 times for Ipswich and enjoyed a great deal of success in his 16 years at Portman Road, plumped for a game in which he finished on the losing side? The answer is simple – I played the greatest game of my life at Old Trafford half a century ago and it is the one game that I remember above all others as I reflect on a wonderful one-club career.

I remember, too, the fact that Manchester United were the finest team in the country, that it was a privilege to share the same pitch as some of the best players in the world at the time. Yes, that's right, the world. Not only were they among the very best in Britain, they were capable of going any-where, and playing any team, and putting on a show. They were so good that they could have dominated our game for years to come. But on that particular day, for many different reasons, we were not far behind them and came very close to causing one of the biggest FA Cup upsets of all time.

Within 12 days of playing at Old Trafford against such formidable oppo-nents we were all plunged into a state of immense shock when we heard what had happened on the runway at Munich Airport. Four of the players who lined up against us – Roger Byrne, Eddie Colman, Mark Jones and Tommy Taylor – were dead along with another three United players – Billy Whelan, Geoff Bent and David Pegg. Worse was to follow when we learned that the death toll had risen to eight with the news that the immensely tal-ented Duncan Edwards, who was only 21 at the time and had been clinging to life for several days, subsequently lost his battle.

I have a number of old scrapbooks and in one of them is pasted a news-paper cutting headlined Great Show, Elsworthy! I have no idea of the paper in which it appeared but it features the by-line of a journalist called Arnold Howe and I would like to share with you exactly what he wrote:

> On the day, long John Elsworthy was a better left-half than Duncan Edwards, England's first choice.
>
> And as Edwards was by no means off form it made me think that it is high time the 6ft. 3in. Nantyderry boy was on the Welsh World Cup short list.

"John was great," said manager Alf Ramsey, the soccer perfectionist. "But I thought all of our boys played well. I'm proud of them."

Alf had good reason to feel happy about his team's display of cultured football at the home of Britain's best.

But the difference between United and Ipswich was adaptability. The Ipswich short passing game looked great – until it became bogged in the Old Trafford mud.

It was then that power play was essential and it was the Manchester men who switched it on.

Elsworthy and skipper Reg Pickett were booting or taking the ball firmly through, but the forwards seemed too keen on seeing the whites of Harry Gregg's eyes before trying a shot.

Ipswich didn't have a Bobby Charlton. The Manchester inside-left had two early chances and fluffed them.

But the next two were goals, both rocket-like affairs that must have strained the net.

Ipswich cannot be counted out of the promotion hunt if they maintain that brand of football.

It is certainly not an in-depth, blow-by-blow account of what happened on the day but the reporter made a number of valid points and for me to even be mentioned in the same breath as Duncan Edwards, never mind the fact that at least one person present thought I played better than him on the day, I consider to be quite an accolade. That he and seven of his colleagues perished at Munich was an absolute tragedy, not forgetting that another 15 people also lost their lives, including one of my own boyhood heroes, the former Manchester City and England goalkeeper Frank Swift, who by that time had retired from playing and was one of the country's best known sports journalists, representing the News of the World.

As a young boy back in Wales I used to watch my local side, Newport County, and I remember two games before the outbreak of the Second World War – against Manchester City and Huddersfield Town, who had Frank Swift and Peter Doherty respectively playing for them. They were my two heroes. Doherty was the greatest player I ever saw, while Swift was the best keeper. I used to think he was out of this world, at least until Gordon Banks came along. Ironically, Frank Swift was at Old Trafford for our game and had some kind things to say about me, and I also have a cutting from the Manchester Evening News 'Pink', whose reporter wrote:

> "Ipswich earned the praise of the crowd at Old Trafford today. They may have been a little lucky at times but no one could dispute their earnestness. Their defence was magnificent and they had one of the outstanding stars in Elsworthy, a brilliant wing half back who was equally dangerous when he moved into attack."

Incidentally, that report also reveals that the gate receipts on the day totalled £7,286, which illustrates how admission prices, and not just players' wages, have risen considerably over the past 50 years. There is another report in my scrapbook under the headline Ipswich Go Down To Champions With Colours Flying, written by an Old International, whoever that might have been, and this is an extract:

> "Elsworthy, at left half, until he tired, and until the goalkeeper, Bailey, was called to a glorious martyrdom in the second half, was the Ipswich player who most captured the imagination.
> "Though having plenty on his plate in having to try to checkmate the dangerous thrusts of Charlton, he had time to spare to initiate all manner of attacking moves on the left flank, and but for a lucky mischance would have had the honour of scoring the opening goal himself.
> "All things considered it was a highly commendable show. Even Edwards could learn much from Elsworthy in the art of placing a ball in a mud patch, of giving it air but not too much, of circumventing an opposing back by chipping the ball over his head."

There were also special mentions for our goalkeeper, Roy Bailey, full backs Basil Acres and Ken Malcolm, centre half Dai Rees and right half Reg Pickett, which might suggest it was a backs to the wall display by Ipswich, although the same report mentions that the second half was ushered in by a shot from Jimmy Leadbetter that struck a post and that the same player suffered a similar fate 10 minutes from the end, this time seeing his shot rebound off the other upright. It was a shame for Jimmy that one of his shots didn't find the net because he was celebrating a career landmark at Old Trafford that day – his 100th first team game for the club

We – my Ipswich team-mates and I – were both disappointed and delighted at the same time when the final whistle sounded. Obviously, we didn't like losing, but we knew we had turned in a good performance and there was no disgrace in going down to such a terrific side. It hardly seemed possible that so soon after we played at Old Trafford so many of the players were dead. We were devastated to hear the first news of the Munich disaster on the radio in the Portman Road dressing room. It was as if we were in a trance and some of us took it really badly with a few tears being shed.

They were such wonderful players, the United boys, and we couldn't quite believe what we were hearing. To lose men in their prime like that was a real tragedy. Great, great players, all of them. They were as good a side as you could ever imagine. Roger Byrne was the United captain. He was quick; in fact in my eyes he was perfect. The day we played them at Old Trafford I thought he was the best player on the field. And Tommy Taylor – there was a bit of Tommy Lawton about him. He had that ability to hang in the air. When he got up he just seemed to stay there. Edwards was a tremendous talent, such a big, strong lad. He had the perfect physique and you could see he was going to be a great player.

Byrne, Taylor and Edwards were all England internationals and Bobby Charlton, whose two goals beat us on the day and who was to eventually win 106 caps, had still to play for his country. He wasn't very old at the time, but the potential was there alright. That burst of speed and an explosive shot in either foot. He was special. You know, these players were all special. Not just for their talent, but they were also gentlemen and genuinely nice people. It was a real pleasure to know them. I found myself chatting to Bobby when we left the pitch that day. Not a long conversation, just a few words. He was fair and admitted United were fortunate.

I remember him saying 'the ball ran for us' and he wished us all the best. That was it. These days you would swap shirts but there was none of that in our time. Then you would all get together and have a drink in the players' lounge but that facility didn't exist then. We didn't mingle with the opposition – we just went to our dressing rooms and then went our separate ways. It never entered my head that I would never see some of those boys again.

It was the very first time that Ipswich met Manchester United. We were in the Second Division, while they had won the First Division in each of the previous two seasons, and at that particular time I doubt if anyone was thinking that within just four years Ipswich would not only occupy a place at the same level but would actually be crowned champions with United down in 15th place. In a reasonably short space of time we not only caught them up but overtook them, which was a massive tribute to Alf and the players he assembled into a title-winning side. When you consider we were a Third Division (South) side in 1957, then finished eighth in the Second Division in 1958, 16th in 1959, 11th in 1960, top in 1961 and then won the First Division in 1962, it was an incredible success story for which Alf deserved the lion's share of the credit.

It was also the biggest crowd that Ipswich had played in front of, so you can probably appreciate what an occasion it was for the players. The supporters, too, made the most of their first chance to see us in action against the famous Manchester United. There were about 3,000 in total and four special trains carried about 1,600 of them, while hundreds of others travelled by road, mainly in a fleet of buses, but some by car. The big problem was the weather and for a time it seemed the game would have to be postponed after a blanket of snow nine inches thick covered the Old Trafford playing surface. They got to work on it on the Thursday morning, using three bulldozers and about 100 men. United rang Ipswich and said that as far as they were concerned the game would go ahead so we left the railway station on the Friday to head up there as the operation to make the pitch playable got into full swing. By Friday night they had virtually removed 500 tons of snow and dumped tons of sand on it. The floodlights were left on overnight to help the thawing process but it rained on the Saturday morning and right up to kick-off time there were people with forks trying to get rid of surface water.

When we got to the ground the other players went out to look at the pitch but I stayed in the dressing room. I just thought I would see enough of the pitch when I went out for the game and didn't see the point in having a look beforehand. You'll never guess what happened next – I fell asleep! It sounds crazy, but I really did dose off. I was sitting on a bench, thinking how different the facilities were to the old cricket pavilion we had at Portman Road, and the next I knew was that I could feel a presence near me. I woke up and who should it be but Alf. He was standing there looking straight at me. He just grinned and said 'I hope you'll be more awake when you get out there'.

It didn't take long for the pitch to churn up and pretty soon it was like a quagmire – 'black porridge' according to one newspaper account. It wouldn't be passed playable nowadays but everybody seemed keen for it to go ahead. It probably had something to do with the distance between the clubs. Travelling wasn't easy in those days and an awful lot of people had set off from Suffolk. I don't think they wanted to postpone it because it would have meant another long trip for the players, never mind the supporters.

People said the pitch was a leveller, which I can understand. After all, we were a Second Division side and they were the best team in Europe. But in truth the conditions also hindered us because we couldn't play our normal game either. Don't forget, we were used to playing on a perfect pitch, probably the best in the country, at Portman Road. Alf made sure we were fired up. There was more devil about us that day and we were more assured. We rose above ourselves and responded to the challenge, although we tired in the last 10 minutes or so and that was when they put the game beyond us.

At the end of the game, when we were back in the dressing room, Alf consoled and comforted us because he knew how well we had done. I often wonder how we might have fared had Ted been fit enough to play. He was an amazing goalscorer and his 41 goals in as many games the previous season had helped us to win the Third Division (South) title. He picked up a knee injury before the 1957-58 season even started and in December he needed to have a cartilage operation, which kept him out again. Typical of Ted, however, he scored 11 goals in the 11 games he did manage to play that season, so you never know if his presence at Old Trafford would have made a difference.

I know one thing – Ted would have relished the opportunity. He was big and strong, so the conditions wouldn't have cramped his style too much. In those days we were encouraged to pass the ball right the way through from the goalkeeper to the front men. Roy Bailey was great at throwing the ball out and I always went looking for it from him. Then I would look for Tom Garneys, another terrific forward, dropping a bit deep and dragging the centre-half with him. Tom would straight away give me the ball back, I would chip it over both him and his marker and by that time Ted would already be getting the other side of them into the space behind them. The full-backs were out wide marking our wingers, who stood right out on the touchline, so there was plenty of space for Ted to exploit. More often than not he would shoot past the keeper or at least force a save from which we would be looking to score on the rebound. We got a lot of goals from that move.

As FAR AS I WAS concerned, I always considered myself very fortunate that I was able to stay with Ipswich throughout my career. Indeed, I counted myself lucky that I had such a long career in the game because there was a time when I was told that I would never play again and had that been the case I would have missed out on an awful lot, including the Second and First Division titles. When I received a kick on my calf at Rotherham one day I thought nothing of it and fully expected to shake it off, even if I knew I would need to receive a bit of treatment. But instead my calf just seemed to get bigger and bigger, and also got redder and redder, to the extent that I had no choice but to tell Alf that I wouldn't be able to play in the next game.

On the Saturday I was in the dressing room and the orthopaedic surgeon, Edward Bell-Jones, came in. He was known to all of us and had performed two cartilage operations on me. He asked me why I wasn't playing and I just showed him my leg. He took one look and said 'Hospital, straight away'. He wanted to call an ambulance but I explained I had travelled to the ground on my bike and wanted to get it home first. When I was cycling up to the house I saw that the ambulance had beaten me to it so I was whisked off to the hospital. I was told I had a blood clot. Apparently, it had been caused by a metal spine in one of my shin guards that had gone into my leg and punctured a vein.

They emphasised that it was life-threatening and I spent three weeks in hospital. Then just before I was due to get discharged Bell-Jones collapsed and died. I didn't know the doctor who came to see me the next day but he was adamant that my career had come to an end. 'You'll never play again' I recall him saying, at which point he handed me two crutches to get myself home. I was living in the grounds of the cemetery at the time with Ann, her parents and our two children, Jane and Martin, who were aged two and one respectively. It was quite a haul back there from Anglesea Road on crutches.

When I went to the ground and let Alf know what I had been told at the hospital he asked if I would like to go to London for a second opinion. I decided instead to go back to the hospital and this time I saw a doctor who had a very different view. He told me it was probably a million to one chance that the same thing would ever happen again and gave me the thumbs-up to continue playing, which was music to my ears after believing I might have played my last game.

THERE WAS A MANCHESTER UNITED connection to me joining Ipswich in 1949. Scott Duncan had been the manager at Old Trafford before joining Ipswich and he had a player called Billy Owen, who was running the Newport youth team when I played in it. They had an arrangement that Billy would tip Scott off about any decent young players he came across and he recommended me. Once Ipswich confirmed I would be joining them Billy asked me to go round to his house and gave me £25 in cash – five lovely white fivers – as a backhander. I'd never seen so much money before. Clearly, Scott had looked after Billy as he had promised to do and Billy thought I was entitled to my share. I used it to buy my very first suitcase, along with a suit and some other clothes, and then a rail ticket to Ipswich. What was left I gave to my dad. I'd never been out of Newport and I didn't have a clue where Ipswich was. I remember the train arriving at Paddington and thinking 'How do I get from here to Liverpool Street?'

Incidentally, Ipswich gave me a signing-on payment on top of the £25 I received from Billy – £10 it was. We didn't earn a fortune but I don't have many regrets about how my career worked out. It would have been nice to have been capped by Wales. Both Dai Rees and I were in the provisional squad of 40 for the World Cup finals in 1958 but neither of us made the cut. The Welsh FA only took 19 players when they were entitled to name a squad of 21 so that didn't help. Funnily enough, there was some confusion for a while as to whether I was Welsh or English. I was adopted as a baby and although I had kept my adoption papers I had no birth certificate. Ann contacted Somerset House in London – without a birth certificate I couldn't get a passport – but had no luck. Fortunately, we had a friend who worked close to Somerset House and he went in one day. He found out quite a lot on our behalf, including the fact that I was definitely born in Wales, which soon put paid to rumours that I might have a chance with England.

There is another reason I consider myself to be a very lucky man. When I was three I had pneumonia and nearly died. In a strange twist of fate, my son had jaundice when he was born in 1958, a week after the game at Old Trafford. It was touch and go for the first three months as to whether Martin would pull through. Ann made a bit of history by becoming the first mother to stay on the children's ward after she refused to leave him overnight. There were no beds for parents so she slept sitting up in a chair at his bedside. There was a threat of brain damage so when they eventually gave him the all-clear it was a huge relief. Years later Ann met the doctor who looked after him and he asked how Martin was doing. 'He's six feet two and a professional golfer,' she told him. The surgeon replied 'My, you were lucky'.

I was originally an inside-left but my game improved when I became a left-half. I could see everything in front of me and really enjoyed the position. It was a pleasure to play with the rest of the players. Alf got us together from all different backgrounds and built us into the best team in the country, which was quite incredible. He was a crafty old so-and-so, mind. Two touches were all he wanted you to take. If the ball came at you chest high he wouldn't let you bring it down on your chest, then trap it and pass it. Oh no, after you chested it down you had to control and pass all in the one movement. That was Alf's rule. I won't hear a word said against him and the members of the World Cup-winning team are the same. He was a perfectionist as a player and he was the same as a manager.

When we won the First Division we were paid 12 shillings and six pence – if my arithmetic is correct that's 62 and a half pence in today's money – for each game we played. I only missed one and when the money came through Ann and I went into town and spent the lot on a washing machine, which was a real luxury at the time.

WHEN THE TIME CAME FOR me to finish – Bill McGarry was the manager by then and I can't pretend that we saw eye to eye – the club awarded Jimmy Leadbetter and I a joint testimonial, and Arsenal came to Portman Road in 1966 for our game, which we won 3-2. After that I concentrated on the grocery business in Foxhall Road, which I had between 1959 and 1969, then I had a post office in Felixstowe Road, which also sold stationery, toys and other items, before I retired.

Like I've said, I consider myself very fortunate. The life of a footballer wasn't anywhere near as glamorous or lucrative as it is today but that didn't stop us enjoying it. We all had our Gladstone bags – they were identical to the ones that doctors carried – and there was no such thing as a team bus. We travelled everywhere by train and after an away match we would arrive back at Ipswich Station to find Ron Ellis waiting for us. Ron was better known as the memory man, a walking encyclopaedia on all things Ipswich, but he kept up his ritual for years. We would all chuck our bags in the back of his van, he would drive to Portman Road and we would walk down there to collect our bikes. If there was such a thing as a player's perk in those days it was that the local bobbies tended to turn a blind eye to the fact that my back light wasn't working as I cycled home late at night!

LARRY CARBERRY
RIGHT-BACK 1956–1965

BORN 18 January 1936, Liverpool
SIGNED 19 May 1956, from amateur
IPSWICH CAREER 285 games
HONOURS Third Division (South) Championship 1956/57; Second
Division 1960/61; First Division 1961/62
LEFT Transferred to Barrow, 30 June 1965

Larry was the only Ipswich Town player to be ever-present in both the
1960/61 and 1961/62 league campaigns as the club followed its Second
Division title success by winning the League Championship at the very first
time of asking. He was in the Army and playing for non-league Bury Town
when he was spotted by Alf Ramsey and in his first season as a professional
he helped Ipswich to become Third Division (South) champions. A model
of consistency, he was close to senior international honours and appeared for
a Football Association X1 on two occasions, as well as being a reserve for the
England Under-23 team. He played for two years with Barrow before he
quit the professional game and combined his job as a docker with playing
part-time for Burscough, where he still lives.

Ipswich Town 4 v Manchester United 1

First Division
Saturday 18 November 1961

Portman Road
Attendance 25,755

Ipswich mark the first-ever league meeting between the sides with a memorable victory that restores them to third place in the First Division table

Teams

Alf Ramsey	**Managers**	Matt Busby
Roy Bailey	1	David Gaskell
Larry Carberry	2	Shay Brennan
John Compton	3	Tony Dunne
Bill Baxter	4	Nobby Stiles
Andy Nelson	5	Bill Foulkes
John Elsworthy	6	Maurice Setters
Dermot Curtis	7	Warren Bradley
Doug Moran	8	Johnny Giles
Ray Crawford	9	David Herd
Ted Phillips	10	Bobby Charlton
Jimmy Leadbetter	11	Sammy McMillan
Phillips 26, 67 Crawford 73, Elsworthy 86	Goals	McMillan 90

Referee: Ken Aston (Ilford)

WHEN WE WON THE Second Division title in 1961 and Ipswich were preparing for life in the First Division for the very first time, the players were every bit as excited as the supporters about what lay ahead. I remember when the fixtures were released we were all looking to see when we would be playing certain sides – the reigning champions, Tottenham, for example – and one of the biggest occasions we were looking forward to was the visit of Manchester United to Portman Road. We had performed very well in an FA Cup-tie at Old Trafford in 1958, a game I missed because I was suffering with flu, but the match I have selected was an historic occasion because it represented the very first time the clubs had met on league business, something that the people who founded Ipswich probably thought would never happen.

Of course, not only had we earned the right to be competing alongside the major clubs, but we also had the beating of most of them that season. I say most of them because there were two, Manchester City and Blackpool, that we didn't manage to defeat on our way to being crowned Champions of England. We lost both times to City – 4-2 at home and 3-0 at Maine Road – while we had two 1-1 draws with Blackpool and I suppose that was a bit strange considering they could only finish 12th and 13th respectively in the table that season. As for United, they were going through a transitional period, having won the title in 1956 and again the next year, only for the Munich tragedy in 1958 to claim the lives of so many of their star players. Manager Matt Busby had to rebuild the team and did a fantastic job, winning the FA Cup in 1963, then the First Division in 1965 and 1967, and the European Cup in 1968.

But there's no doubt about who were top dogs in that unforgettable 1961-62 campaign and we didn't just beat Manchester United at Portman Road, we completely overwhelmed them. To be honest, as I recalled it we won the game 4-0 – I had completely forgotten their goal, which was a mere consolation as it came in the dying seconds. United went the way of most teams who came to our place that year. We could do little wrong in front of our own fans and it was undoubtedly our home form that won us the league. Of our 21 home games we won 17 of them, drew two and lost two, which meant we picked up 36 of our 56 points at Portman Road.

One reason I opted for this particular game is that it coincided with me receiving a benefit from Ipswich. In those days you were given a benefit to mark five years with the club. In the Third Division players would be paid £500 but in both the Second and First Divisions the agreed sum was £750, while in Ipswich's case they also arranged a collection among the crowd, which was done by asking supporters to throw coins into a blanket as it was carried round the pitch at half-time. It doesn't sound like much in comparison to what today's footballers are earning but we all regarded it as a nice perk and back then it was a tidy sum not to be sneezed at.

We had made the top three for the first time that season when we beat Nottingham Forest 1-0 at home – Roy Bailey saved a late penalty that day – and after we went to Wolves and lost 2-0 it was Manchester United next at our place. We were approaching the half-way point in the season and happy about how things were going, but nobody was thinking about the possibility of actually winning the league at that stage. The ground wasn't quite full but there was a tremendous atmosphere and the presence of the England manager, Walter Winterbottom, set a few tongues wagging. There had been some talk of maybe Ray Crawford and Ted Phillips forcing their way into his squad and, sure enough, Ray became the club's first-ever England player a few weeks later, with a lot of people of the belief that Ted should also have been selected.

Ted looked to have done his chances no harm when he scored our first goal, although we should have been further ahead at half-time given the amount of possession we had and the chances we had created. The goals did flow in the second half, however, and Ted netted again to extend our lead. He was close to getting a hat-trick on at least a couple of occasions before Ray weighed in with a third goal, but it was our fourth and final goal, scored by John Elsworthy four minutes from the end, that really brought the house down. We were awarded a free-kick and because we were winning comfortably – we probably should have scored several more goals in the game – he decided to try something different. He played a lot of rugby back home in Wales as a youngster and had learned how to put back-spin on the ball when taking conversions. He applied a similar technique to the football and while it looked as if United goalkeeper David Gaskell had made a terrible blunder, it was actually the spin on the ball that caused it to fly up his arm and over his shoulder into the net.

United got a goal just before the end but they knew they had taken a bit of a hammering and didn't like it one bit. Being a Liverpool fan as a kid, I was absolutely elated, not just by the win and the margin of victory but with the way we had played to get it. I looked at some of the opposition players and it was clear to see they were furious. They had people like Nobby Stiles and Maurice Setters, who were among the most competitive players in the country, but they had no answer to our game. We weren't really an aggressive side, although Bill Baxter was as uncompromising as they came and didn't like anyone getting the better of him. We liked to concentrate on passing the ball and feeding it into our front players, Ray and Ted, and on the day United were simply unable to stop us from recording another famous victory, just one of many that season.

ONE THING THAT DEFINITELY helped us was that we were able to field an unchanged side on so many occasions. We used 16 players in the league that season, but five of them only made a total of 16 appearances between them and most weeks, if we had a clean bill of health, the team virtually picked itself. Not only that, but the team that won the Second Division title virtually stayed together for the new season because Alf Ramsey only added one new player, Doug Moran, in the summer of 1961. Players would also turn out when less than 100 per cent fit – I know I did on occasions – and Alf basically left it to the individuals to decide whether they were going to be okay. Nowadays, with squads so much bigger, players seem quite happy to sit on the bench and pick up their wages. There were no substitutes in those days, of course, and it was just as well because players would have far rather turned out for the reserves than sit on the sidelines. I was one of three players – captain Andy Nelson and Doug Moran were the others – who played every First Division game that season, while four were only missing once and a further two were absent just twice.

I had a lot of very good wingers to mark that season. I remember that three weeks after we beat United we were playing Aston Villa away from home and beforehand Alf said to me 'If you can stop Peter McParland we will win the game.' Unfortunately, I couldn't and he scored twice as we went down 3-0 at Villa Park. I was looking forward to Villa coming to our place so that I could hopefully even the score but McParland didn't play. Mind you, because the return game was on the last day of the season and a 2-0 win earned us the title, I was happy enough. Cliff Jones of Tottenham and Bobby Charlton of United were other top-class wingers I had to mark but in those days every side played with wingers and I had a lot of good tussles. I had a decent turn of pace and could recover quickly but Alf always marked my card about my direct opponent so I was always properly prepared.

It was Alf who came up with the idea of playing our two wingers, Roy Stephenson and Jimmy Leadbetter, in withdrawn positions and that was a tactic that opposition teams struggled to come to terms with. Also, with Alf having been a right-back for Tottenham and England, he gave me a lot of useful advice to help my own game. When I think back more than half a century to when I signed for Ipswich, the truth is that I was actually signing for Alf. It wasn't the money – I collected a £10 signing-on fee – but Alf who won me over in the first place and I never had even the slightest regret about my decision. In my mind he was a genius who was capable of getting the very best out of all his players. Whatever Alf predicted it came off – he told me that within three months of signing full-time I would be in the first team and he also told me I would gain representative honours.

He was right on both counts. I was in the Army and playing as an amateur for the reserves before I signed as a professional in advance of the 1956/57 season. I got into the team in November that year and clocked up 25 league games and a further three in the FA Cup. I ended my first season with a Third Division (South) medal and I was one of five players, along with Roy Bailey, John Elsworthy, Jimmy Leadbetter and Ted Phillips, who were still in the side five years later, by which time we had added Second and First Division medals. I was picked to play for an FA X1 and I was also a reserve for the England Under-23 side for a game against Romania at Wembley. There were three reserves, or substitutes, stripped and ready to go on if required – a goalkeeper called Peter Wakeham, who played for Sunderland and Charlton, the one and only Bobby Charlton and yours truly. I remember Maurice Setters was playing that day and when he went down a couple of times I began to think of getting on. Had it been any other player I may well have done but Maurice was a tough lad and clearly didn't fancy coming off.

All of the players who were with Ipswich in Alf's time in charge owe him a huge debt of gratitude. We were regarded as a team of has-beens and never-was players. Alf saw something in all of us that convinced him he could mould us into a good team. He took players from other clubs, where they were out of the first team picture, and gave them a new lease of life. As far as I was concerned, I found myself in the right place at the right time. I was in the Lancashire Fusiliers and when they disbanded I joined the King's Regiment and was stationed at Bury St Edmunds. I played for Bury Town

– they paid me five shillings per game – but when Alf saw me playing I was actually representing my regiment against Bury. We had a number of players who were signed for clubs up north but were given permission to play for Bury. The strange thing about me meeting Alf at the end of the game was that he had left his seat before the final whistle because he had to get round to the opposite side of the ground. He was waiting with the Bury manager as I came off the pitch. I felt very honoured when I later read in a Sunday newspaper that it was the first time Alf had been known to leave his seat before the end of a game.

The game that Alf attended was on a Tuesday evening and two days later the Ipswich team bus stopped at the Army camp to pick me up and take me up to Leicester for a reserve fixture at Filbert Street. That was the start of a long, successful and very happy association with Ipswich, although I'd no idea at the time just how well things would ultimately work out. Ipswich were not the only club who wanted to sign me but because of Alf I was only interested in joining them. He was a wonderful person, not just a very good manager, and I will always be grateful for the guidance he gave me. He was a true gentleman as well, very fair and loyal to all his players. Alf was good at planning things and he must have had a photographic memory the way he was able to recall absolutely everything that happened in a game, both good and bad. He also had the knack of keeping everything simple and uncomplicated, which the players appreciated.

IT WAS FATE THAT decreed I would sign for Ipswich. I actually had the offer of a trial at Norwich while I was stationed at Bury. I would have gone, too, had it not been for the fact that I was on guard duty and couldn't get there. I did manage to go up to Stoke for a trial and they asked me to come back for a second time. Wilf Hall, who was to become an Ipswich colleague when he was understudy to goalkeeper Roy Bailey, was at Stoke at the time and played a part in getting me up there. Again, however, I was required at Stoke at the same time as I was to be on guard duty and when I showed the sergeant major the letter I had received, hoping he would give me permission to travel up there, he was anything but impressed and insisted the guard duty came first.

Even when Ipswich asked me to sign I had an alternative offer from Liverpool, the team I supported as a kid. My dad just assumed I would be joining Liverpool – he was a supporter as well – and he wasn't amused when I said I had decided to sign for Ipswich. Liverpool were a league higher and obviously closer to home but I stuck to my guns. I just told my dad 'If I don't make it at Ipswich I wouldn't make it at Liverpool.' Little did I realise at the time that Ipswich would be overtaking Liverpool and winning the League Championship. The year we won the Second Division they finished third and the game at Anfield was a highlight for me. We got a 1-1 draw up there and managed to beat them 1-0 at Portman Road, two results that went a long way towards helping us win the league. I got a real kick out of playing at Anfield and it was the same at Goodison Park the following season, even if we lost 5-2. We made up for that result with a 4-0 win at home on our way to winning the First Division and Everton, who finished fourth, succeeded us as champions. Both at Anfield and Goodison, when I was out near the touchline, I could hear comments from the supporters that were directed at me – just good banter because I was a Scouser playing for the opposition.

If my decision to sign for Ipswich rather than Liverpool shocked my father, my family couldn't believe my decision to turn down the job as chief scout at Anfield after my playing career came to a halt at Barrow in 1967. I came home one day and Joe Fagan, a key member of Bill Shankly's back-room team and future Liverpool manager, was sitting in my front room. He said Shanks had sent him to ask me to pop down to the club for a chat. When I met up with Shanks he said he wanted me to take over from Norman Low, a former Norwich manager, who was going off to the United States. Norman wasn't going for another eight weeks and Shanks suggest-ed I come down to the club a few times a week to see what I thought. I went backwards and forwards until Shanks said he needed a decision from me and I declined.

When they heard what I had decided my relatives and my workmates on the docks all thought I was mad. I soon realised why when they admitted I would have been their first port of call for tickets to the big games. I turned the job down because I wondered what would happen if they had a change of manager and I honestly thought the docks was a more secure alternative. The important thing is that I don't look back with any regrets, even if some family members might not have forgiven me. My team was always Liverpool and two of my four children, Mary and David, have taken after me. But my wife Mary's family leaned towards Everton and that has influ-enced my other two kids, Lawrence and John. It's not unusual – football has divided plenty of families on Merseyside over the years.

Ipswich's away game against Liverpool in January 1961 wasn't my first experience of playing at Anfield. I'd actually played there on two previous occasions as a youngster. We had 13,000 people turn up at a schools' cup final there and I also played for a youth select against the Liverpool youth side, which was an annual fixture at the time and followed a trip to Holland and Germany by the select squad. After that game I was walking away from the ground with my dad and an uncle when we were approached by an Everton scout. My dad was a Liverpool fan but my uncle supported Everton, so you can probably picture the scene. I ended up playing for the Everton A team but I didn't enjoy it. Some of the lads had been with England and it just wasn't my cup of tea so I packed it in and went back to playing for my local youth team.

I AM ONE OF FIVE KIDS raised in the Scotland Road area and virtual-ly all the boys wanted to play professional football. Some, me included, were lucky and made a good living out of the game, while others fell by the wayside. It was a very close-knit working class community and is also famous for the fact that Cilla Black and the actor Tom Baker, probably best known for playing Doctor Who, also grew up there. I played in the same school team as two lads who went on to play for Liverpool – Jimmy Melia and Bobby Campbell. Later in life Jimmy was famous for leading Brighton to the FA Cup Final in 1990, when they lost to Manchester United in a replay, while Bobby managed Fulham, Portsmouth and Chelsea. But we had our very own claim to fame in 1962, because while I was picking up my First Division winner's medal, Jimmy was collecting a Second Division version with Liverpool and Bobby a Third Division (South) medal with Pompey. Not bad for three kids from the Scottie Road, where we first kicked a ball around on the cobbled streets and Second World War bomb sites!

I was actually recommended to Liverpool by one of their own players, Ronnie Moran, who had a very long and successful association with the club after his playing days were over and he joined the coaching staff to work with Bill Shankly, Bob Paisley, Joe Fagan, Kenny Dalglish and others. It was after I played against Ronnie in the Army that he told Anfield manager Don Welsh about me. Ronnie was actually a left-back and if I'd signed we might have gone on to form a defensive partnership. As I've said, though, I couldn't turn Alf down. I signed for him, rather than Ipswich, and I don't think I could have had a better football education. When I look back on my time at Portman Road I feel very privileged to have worked for such a great man.

There's one Alf Ramsey story that tends to sum him up. In February 1959, when we were in the bottom half of the Second Division, we were about to play Luton in the fifth round of the FA Cup at Portman Road. They were a First Division club then and we knew the tie would attract a big crowd so there was a fair bit of talk beforehand about bonus payments. Nothing was agreed and the talk was even going on in the dressing room less than an hour before the kick-off. I was one of the quiet ones but others were more vociferous and there was even a suggestion that we might not play the game unless certain financial issues were resolved there and then. 'In that case I shall go and tell them there won't be a game today,' said Alf, knowing full well we would not refuse to fulfil the fixture. There was no way Alf was going to give in and instead he called the players' bluff and let everyone know who was in charge. We were 4-1 down at half-time in that game and although we pulled our sleeves up in the second half we were beaten 5-2 in the end. Luton went on to reach the final but lost to Nottingham Forest at Wembley.

Life could have taken me in a very different direction had I not quit my apprenticeship as a joiner then taken a job as a sheet metal worker before doing my national service in the Army and being posted to Suffolk. Who knows what the future might have held had I been sent somewhere else? I settled in really well at Portman Road and I think the team appreciated my younger legs. The right-halves in those days were Neil Myles and Reg Pickett, who were quite happy for me to go forward. I knew they weren't going anywhere so I was always prepared to take the chance of pushing on. One of Alf's mottos was 'If you start a move, follow it up'. Ted Phillips banged in 41 goals in the same number of league games in my first season, but it didn't surprise me. He had been sent out to Stowmarket the previous season and I played against him for Bury. Our manager would always tell us the same thing before we played Stowmarket – 'Stop Phillips and we stop them' – but it was easier said than done and Ted was still scoring for fun when we won the First Division.

One of our biggest strengths at Ipswich was the camaraderie, the team spirit. We had no prima donnas in the team. We were a very close-knit bunch – Alf went out of his way to ensure that – and we got on very well both on and off the field of play. My best pal was Jimmy Leadbetter and we always roomed together on the away trips when an overnight stay was required. Some players didn't want to share a room with Jimmy because they complained he was always reading and they had trouble getting a conversation out of him. But I didn't mind. Jimmy would lie on his bed reading and I was the type who could just put his head on the pillow and instantly fall asleep. Perfect partners, we were. Our wives also became great friends.

I was honoured, when I attended the annual reunion dinner in March 2008, to collect Jimmy's trophy for being inducted into the club's Hall of Fame. My wife, Mary, and I were intending to take it up to Edinburgh in the summer and hand it over to his widow, Janet, but less than three weeks after the dinner we received a call from Jimmy and Janet's daughter, Shirley, with the terrible news that her mother had passed away. We attended the funeral and gave the trophy to Shirley, who was very proud of her father and what he achieved.

Talking of children, two of my boys, David and John, showed a lot of ability as youngsters, to the extent that both were associated with Manchester United. David was a very quick centre-forward and after a few games for the A team he was promoted to the reserves, where he played alongside Mark Hughes and Norman Whiteside, and averaged better than a goal per game. Unfortunately, he required no fewer than three cartilage operations, and also broke a toe, within the space of a year. He was never the same after that and ended up playing non-league football of a decent standard. In John's case he was playing for United's youth team but after going on holiday to Spain with some friends he collapsed with a mystery illness that turned out to have affected his pancreas. His weight plummeted by a couple of stone in a fortnight and it took him nearly two years to make a proper recovery, by which time his chance had gone. Just as fate decreed that I would join Ipswich and go on to win a League Championship medal, it wasn't anywhere near as kind to my boys. More recently, John has been running the Lancashire county side.

I MENTIONED THE CAMARADERIE that existed at Portman Road and it was the same when I worked on the docks. Every summer we would lock up the house in Ipswich and go back to Liverpool, where I had a summer job on the docks. There was nothing unusual about it – all the players did it. Some would work at the brewery, in timber yards or on farms, or in Ray Crawford's case the furniture department at the local Co-op store. I worked on the docks unloading fruit cargoes from all over the world and I loved it. Even after picking up my First Division winner's medal in 1962 I went back home to work on the docks that summer. When my professional playing career came to an end at Barrow, and I decided the job as chief scout at Liverpool wasn't for me, I went to work full-time at the docks for almost 20 years before I retired. Happy days!

I went on to become player-manager of Burscough – I actually had three spells in charge because I tended to look after them while they were in between managers – and I realised how much Alf had taught me about management. He very rarely raised his voice and never, ever swore in all the time I played for him at Ipswich. If we lost and things hadn't gone well he would say 'What went wrong boys?' and immediately set about putting things right for the next game. Right at the start of my time as a full-time pro at the club, when I was in the reserves, the first team were really struggling to pick up points. There was no panic from Alf, who stayed perfectly calm and assured the players things would improve. And he was right – we went from the bottom of the league to the very top and I collected a Third Division (South) winner's medal within a few months of my debut.

It's just possible that one of my grandsons, Adam Blakeman, could follow in my footsteps. He was with the Liverpool academy for about six or seven years and in 2008 moved over to Bolton, where he played for the Under-18 side despite only being 16, His brother, Liam, was in the Blackburn youth team when they lost 6-3 over two legs to Arsenal in the 2001 FA Youth Cup Final and then he played for Burscough when they beat Gillingham in the first round of the FA Cup in December 2005. His father – my son-in-law Alex – also played for Burscough at the same stage of the competition in 1979 and there has been a long association between Burscough and the Carberry clan. At the time of writing Liam is with Southport, for whom he has played in virtually every position and even had a stint as an emergency goalkeeper.

TED PHILLIPS
INSIDE-FORWARD 1953–1964

BORN 21 August 1933, Snape, Suffolk
SIGNED 11 December 1953 from Leiston Town
IPSWICH CAREER 295 games, 181 goals
HONOURS Third Division (South) Championship 1956/57; Second Division 1960/61; First Division 1961/62
LEFT Transferred to Leyton Orient, 16 March 1964

Ted is the only player in Ipswich Town's history to score more goals in a season than games played. He did it in the 1956/57 campaign, netting 46 times in 44 games, a phenomenal record that helped the club to capture the Third Division (South) crown and made him the leading marksman in the entire Football League. Ted's goals – 30 in as many games – continued to be invaluable as Ipswich won the Second Division crown in 1960/61 and the following year he was on target 36 times in 50 league and cup appearances as Town were crowned Champions of England. He was credited with the hardest shot in football and his partnership with Ray Crawford in that fabulous era was the most prolific in the club's history. He later played for Leyton Orient, Luton and Colchester, and was also player-manager of Maltese club Floriana. He is retired and lives in Colchester.

Tottenham Hotspur 1 v Ipswich Town 3

First Division
Wednesday 14 March 1962

White Hart Lane
Attendance 51,098

Alf Ramsey makes a triumphant return to his former club and Ipswich complete the double over the reigning champions en route to proving themselves worthy successors

Teams

Bill Nicholson	**Managers**	Alf Ramsey
Bill Brown	1	Roy Bailey
Peter Baker	2	Larry Carberry
Ron Henry	3	John Compton
Danny Blanchflower	4	Bill Baxter
Maurice Norman	5	Andy Nelson
Tony Marchi	6	John Elsworthy
Cliff Jones	7	Roy Stephenson
John White	8	Doug Moran
Bobby Smith	9	Ray Crawford
Jimmy Greaves	10	Ted Phillips
Terry Medwin	11	Jimmy Leadbetter
Greaves 9	Goals	Crawford 8, Phillips 41, 71

Referee: W Haynes (Lancashire)

WHEN IPSWICH BEAT TOTTENHAM at White Hart Lane it was widely acknowledged, at the time, as the best result in the club's history. As the reigning champions, all the others were out to topple Spurs, and because they were the first winners in the modern area of the League and FA Cup double, which they had achieved less than a year earlier, there was an even greater incentive to beat them. For us to defeat them on their own patch, having already beaten them at Portman Road earlier in that unforgettable season, was considered a magnificent achievement and went a long way towards us inheriting their league title. I remember how it brought a huge smile to the face of our manager, Alf Ramsey, who could not conceal his delight at returning to his former club and claiming a victory that was thoroughly deserved. The win also underlined the fact that we were genuine title contenders and simply had to be taken seriously, something a lot of critics had been reluctant to do until then.

It was a big, big game and I know a lot of Ipswich supporters who attended, including some people who were youngsters at the time and went on a coach trip organised by their school. Others travelled on a fleet of coaches or by special train from Ipswich to Northumberland Park and to this day they talk about it as one of the very special occasions in their time following the club. It is also interesting that in those days they were able to choose which part of the ground they entered. There was no such thing as segregation, nor was there any sign of trouble as opposition fans rubbed shoulders with one another in a capacity crowd, although I dare say the Ipswich supporters had to put up with the usual 'country bumpkin' taunts.

One thing I remember about the game that was different to all the others we played in London over the years was that Alf organised a coach to meet the train from Ipswich and take us from Liverpool Street to the stadium. It might be hard to believe now, with teams tending to travel everywhere by luxury coach or chartered plane, but we would usually travel by rail and then hop on the underground to wherever we were playing. We were expected to pay our own fares, too, although the club reimbursed us later on. I lived in Colchester back then – my wife Diane and I are still in the same house – and I recall getting a lift down to the station to meet the train from Ipswich. I met the others in the restaurant car because the club had booked us a meal, which we had in good time before arriving in London.

Alf left us in no doubt as to the importance of the game and we could tell that it would mean a lot to him if we won it. We got off to a brilliant start when Ray Crawford got through to put us into an early lead but we were pegged back virtually straight away when Jimmy Greaves equalised. In and around the box Greavsie was the best in the business, but thankfully we managed to keep him quiet after that, something that very few teams could do at that time. If I remember rightly, I put us back in front just before half-time with a header when I outjumped their big centre-half, Maurice Norman. He knocked me for six as I got my head to it but the main thing was that the ball ended up in the back of the net. I actually preferred my second goal – a typical Ted Phillips goal if you like – when Doug Moran put me through and I had to run about 40 yards from the half-way line. Doug was a clever player, the type who was aware of everything that was going on around him, and he won a challenge before slipping the ball through perfectly.

I was aware of being in the clear and everyone chasing me, but over that sort of distance I was probably the quickest player at the club and there was no way anyone was going to catch me. I looked up and saw Bill Brown, their Scottish international goalkeeper, come out towards me and I was still going at full pelt. Suddenly, Brown not only stopped but started to back away and at that precise moment, when I was just outside the 18-yard box, I decided to hit it. The ball flew past Brown – in fact I think he went the wrong way for my shot and didn't even see the ball – and we were 3-1 ahead. The thing I remember most about that situation was the way Spurs captain Danny Blanchflower had a right go at Brown for backing off as I ran through. He swore at him and even called him a coward, at which point the referee blew his whistle and said 'Enough of that, Danny. Save that sort of thing for when you are on television.' That was a reference to the fact that Danny was one of the very first TV pundits and wasn't shy when it came to giving his opinion.

To score two goals was great but I could, and probably should, have had a hat-trick that night. It would have been a perfect hat-trick, too, because I'd already scored with a header and a right-foot shot when, later on, I had a go with my left foot and the ball hit the junction of bar and post. It was an awkward chance in a way, because the ball was in the air and I couldn't really afford to let it come down, but I still felt I should have scored. The main thing was that we won and to be honest we were never really in danger of losing, or even drawing, the game. A pal of mine who was there, and who attended most of our games in that era, said to me afterwards that he had never seen me play a better game for Ipswich. I confess I didn't come off the pitch thinking it was my best-ever game, although I knew I had played well, but maybe my friend was right. I wasn't one to blow my own trumpet – I preferred to leave it to Alf to dish out the praise.

Alf was waiting for us as we came into the dressing room at White Hart Lane and he made a point of congratulating each and every one of us, patting us all on the back. He looked as if he had won the pools, he was so happy. It clearly meant a lot for him to go back to his old club and win. Not only that, but we completed a league double over them that season. It was a great achievement to beat the reigning champions at our own place but to go to London and turn them over really was something else.

Spurs were known for their push-and-run style of play and Alf clearly learned a lot from his time with them. He went straight into management after he retired as a player and I remember how he would be on the phone most Monday mornings to the Spurs manager, Arthur Rowe, talking football and picking his brains. Bill Nicholson was the manager when we beat them that night, of course, and a home defeat was anything but a normal occurrence for his team. After the game we walked out of the ground and straight into the first pub we found, which was virtually next door. The chairman, Mr John (Cobbold), virtually insisted we went in and he bought the first round. The place was full of Spurs' fans but we went into the posh bit, the lounge, and there was no trouble. Imagine that happening now – well it wouldn't, would it? Alf didn't like the way Mr John would take the players for a drink, but he couldn't stop him. You heard Mr John before you saw him because he had so many whisky miniatures in his coat pockets. I remember Alf standing there shouting 'Come on lads' and I said 'Not likely, I've still got a pint here.' We'd have stayed all night if we could have done but Alf eventually dragged us out and on to the bus to get to Liverpool Street just in time for the last train.

PERSONALLY, THE WIN AT Spurs meant a great deal to me because it came after I'd had a very lean time of it goals-wise. I scored 20 in our first 19 league games that season but then they dried up for a spell. It can happen to the best of us and in my next seven I didn't manage a single goal. Then I got two in my next three but another couple of blanks meant I had only scored twice in 12 league games before the game at Tottenham. I wasn't over-concerned because Alf was keeping faith in me, plus I had also scored three goals in the same number of FA Cup-ties against Luton. I also had influenza and one or two niggling injuries, and you tended to get on with it in those days – unless, of course, it was something really serious.

Unfortunately, some people weren't prepared to let the situation be. The local paper called for me to be dropped and some supporters voiced their disapproval in no uncertain terms. It was normally water off a duck's back to me, although I snapped on one occasion at Portman Road when I heard a supporter shout 'Wake yourself up, Phillips.' It was at the Churchmans end of the ground and I could see the culprit, so I peeled my shirt off and made to hand it over to him. 'Here you go, mate,' I said. 'See if you can do any better.' The chap looked a bit embarrassed as I pulled the shirt back and put it on again. I can't remember who we were playing that day but needless to say I got into hot water with Alf afterwards. He gave me a right good rollicking in the dressing room and warned me never to do the same thing again. In those days players weren't allowed to drive cars – it was deemed too dangerous – so I used to have a policeman pal of mine called Terry Roberts who would drive me to games. Afterwards, as we were walking towards the car, the same chap who had shouted at me during the game came up and apologised, which I thought was pretty decent of him.

To go into the game at Tottenham with such a poor return in terms of goals wasn't really a big deal to me. I'd been around long enough to know that the bad run wouldn't last for ever, so to get two and come close to a hat-trick was a great feeling. I hoped I would be on a roll but in my very next game I broke a thumb. It was against Blackpool at Portman Road and it was a real anti-climax after the win at Spurs just a few days earlier. We got a great welcome from the fans but we conceded a goal just before the end and had to settle for a 1-1 draw. I missed two games and returned to score four times in our last seven games, which took my end-of-season league tally to 28 from 40 games, although with FA Cup and League Cup games included I actually scored 36 from 50 games. Most importantly, of course, we were the Champions of England ahead of runners-up Burnley and Tottenham, who had to settle for third place with four points fewer than ourselves.

I could hardly believe I had won a League Championship medal to go with the Second Division one I had picked up just 12 months earlier. I went into football and never gave it a second thought that I would get a medal of any sort, never mind the one that every player wanted. Mind you, virtually the whole country was stunned by our achievement. We started the season as favourites to go straight back down again, only for the very opposite to happen. Ray (Crawford) was top scorer with 33 goals in 41 league games – 37 from 50 including cup-ties, which meant we were separated by just the one goal. A lot of Ray's goals came on the rebound from my shots, which he never denied, but in fairness to him he was the best I ever saw when it came to following up and taking advantage of any slips by the keeper.

I collected my first medal in 1956-57 when we won the Third Division (South) and I scored 41 goals in 41 league games. I also scored five times in three FA Cup-ties so my final total was 46 from 44 games. But the most amazing thing about that season was that we literally went from the bottom to the top of the table, having won just one of our first nine games and taking just four points from a possible 18. It was after I completed my national service in the Army that I had signed for Ipswich towards the end of 1953 from my local club, Leiston, and I spent the 1955-56 season with Stowmarket in the Eastern Counties League. The idea was to get myself fully fit after I had picked up a knee injury in pre-season training at HMS Ganges, which was out at Shotley.

My manager at Leiston was a chap called Ian Gillespie and he rang the club to recommend me. The manager back then was Scott Duncan and he arranged for me to go down to Portman Road one day. I had to get time off from my job with the Forestry Commission. I was told to get my boots on and get out on to the practice pitch. I remember how the trainer, Jimmy Forsyth, brought a huge bag of balls out with him. Scott had asked Billy Reed, the right-winger, and Tom Garneys, the centre-forward, to help out. Billy crossed the ball, Tom headed it down and I whacked it into the net. I'd had about 20 shots when Scott called me off. He must have been impressed because the following Sunday I was woken up quite early and there was Scott at the front door to get me to sign the forms.

Scott's team talks were never very long. He would say 'You full-backs, get the ball up to the wingers. You wingers, get it over to the forwards. And you forwards, stick it in the net.' Then he would pour himself a glass of port and that was it. Alf was nothing like that. He could talk anyone into playing football. He was so organised that I swear he could think up free-kick routines in his sleep. We would spend three hours training on a Friday and most of the time was spent working on a new routine he had dreamed up. Mind you, when we went out the next day and tried it out in the game it invariably worked and we scored. Alf could make a team talk last a couple of hours, he was so thorough. I'd have been nothing without Alf. He made me as a player the way he chatted to me and built up my confidence. He was like a god to me.

EVERYBODY HAS THEIR ALF stories and I've a few. I think the one that best summed him up was when we were passengers on the same train out of London one day. I had been working up there laying cables and he was the England manager. We sat together until I got off in Colchester. He even went off to the refreshment carriage and bought us some drinks. We had a right good chat and he seemed fine. It was only the next morning, when my newspaper was delivered, that I learned Alf had been sacked by the Football Association the previous day. Clearly, he had come straight to the station from being told the terrible news at FA headquarters in Lancaster Gate. When we met each other on the train right up until I got off at Colchester he never said a thing. But when I thought about it later I wasn't that surprised, because he was a very private man.

They were great times at Ipswich and if Alf and I had words from time to time it was never anything serious. Mind you, he wasn't very pleased when I asked for a transfer one season. Liverpool, West Ham and even Rangers up in Scotland were all keen to sign me but Alf just kept saying I wasn't for sale and that was the end of it. He loved to talk football but wasn't really interested in chatting about anything else. Ray and I proved it one day when we were sat with him. We agreed we would change the subject and see what happened. Suddenly, I said to Ray 'What do you think of the new Vauxhall?' and, sure enough, Alf just got up and walked away. Alf had a thing about training without a ball and it used to wind me up to the point where I would get a hold of balls and hide them in different areas of the ground. I loved my shooting practice, you see, so when training finished I would get hold of the balls and have my own session. Alf couldn't figure out where I kept the balls and even had people following me to see if he could find out. But he never did.

I had a reputation for practical jokes and I think my favourite was the day when we were all sitting down to a meal at a hotel before an away game. They were passing the soup down the table to the far end and I worked out which one would be Alf's and slipped a plastic cockroach into it. Sure enough, just as I knew he would, Alf complained and a waiter came along to point out that it wasn't real. Alf just looked up and shouted 'Phillips!' He knew exactly who had done it. He liked to take us out to the pictures on a Friday night when we had to travel overnight for a game and on one occasion, when we were up north, three of us slipped out of the cinema soon after the film started. We went off and found a pub to have a drink and returned for the last few minutes. We were sat a few rows behind Alf and thought we had fooled him. But on the way back to the hotel he came up to me and asked what I thought of the film. He just smiled as I attempted an answer and it was clear I'd been rumbled again. But the same Alf had me in his office one day after Ray had been called up by England and told me 'You should be there with him, Ted,' which meant a great deal to me.

Our trainer, Jimmy Forsyth, was on the receiving end of a few of my pranks. He was a good sport. I put some bricks in his bag one day when we were at the station and he could hardly lift it off the platform. Another time I put British Rail cutlery in his coat pocket and when he put it on the knives, forks and spoons went everywhere, making a terrible noise. But one joke very nearly backfired. We were in London waiting to head north when I jumped up and said 'This is our train, Jimmy.' I even helped him on with the skip, then I quickly hopped off again and the train pulled away with him on it and the rest of us standing on the platform. Jimmy ended up in Preston but we were actually playing at Stoke and he only got to the ground with 20 minutes to spare.

One of the funniest things I ever saw was when we got the train to London for a game and we were on the tube heading for the ground. We had to stand because it was so busy and Alf was hanging on to keep his balance when this bloke got on at a station and spotted him. He was a real cockney and said 'Alfie boy, how are you?' Alf said nothing. The bloke tried again when he said 'Don't you remember me, Alfie? I went to school with you.' Still nothing from Alf. We had to get off a couple of stops later and as we were going up the steps I said to Alf 'Who was that bloke on the train? He reckoned he went to school with you.' Alf just said in that posh sort of voice of his 'I've never seen him before in my life' and made it clear that was the end of the conversation.

Maybe it was because I got into so many scrapes as a youngster – and lived to tell the tale – that I liked to have a laugh. There was even an occasion when I disappeared down a well at our house and it was one of my three brothers who raised the alarm. My mother was able to get some builders, who were putting up council houses nearby, to come and get me out. I also had double pneumonia as a child and they didn't expect me to pull through. I even heard them say 'He's a goner' but I had hot poultices applied every day for weeks and eventually beat it. I was left with a white patch of hair at the back of my head as a reminder of the illness, a distinguishing mark that provoked a few comments when I was playing and is still there to this day

My pace and strength were great talents, but my ability to hit the ball so hard was definitely my biggest asset. Most people probably assumed it was a God-given talent but my theory is rather different. As a youngster setting off on the walk to school every morning, I always had a tennis ball in my pocket. I would get it out and kick it all the way there and back, as well as playing with it in the playground in between. Eventually I kicked my shoes to pieces and because there wasn't enough money to buy me another pair I had no alternative but to go to school in my socks. One of my brothers would carry me as far as he could but I still wanted to kick the ball and I genuinely believe that's what toughened up my feet.

I had the strongest shot in football at one time – 87 miles an hour it was measured at – and that was with a big heavy leather ball that would absorb water. A national newspaper organised a competition and they had equipment rigged up at Tottenham's training ground. Spurs had the England centre-forward at the time, Bobby Smith, and he took part against me. The idea was that we had to shoot at a target about three feet square. We had six shots each but Bobby only hit it once. But I'm the first to admit that being blessed with such a powerful shot would have counted for little if I hadn't had such good players alongside me at Ipswich. Jimmy (Leadbetter), Doug (Moran), big John (Elsworthy) and Roy (Stephenson) were all brilliant at threading the ball through. Alf taught me a lot about timing my runs and the other players' passing ability counted for a lot as well.

After Ipswich I played for Leyton Orient, Luton and Colchester, where I fell out with manager Neil Franklin because he refused me permission to play for Suffolk at cricket, another sport at which I was pretty good as a fast bowler. Out of the blue, I received an offer to go over to Malta and become the player-manager of Floriana, the team we had knocked out of the European Cup in 1962. I asked Alf's advice and he said I should go, plus the money they were offering was really too good to turn down. I was over there for just over a year, during which time we won the cup, and when my wife and I went on a Mediterranean cruise early in 2008 we were able to visit the flat in Valletta that was our home. When I came back from Malta I had a spell with Chelmsford before I finished completely with football. Over the years I have had to have two new knees and it has caused me to stop going to Portman Road because I cannot sit comfortably in the modern seating, although I make a point of attending the annual reunion dinner organised by the club.

The way football has changed since I played for Ipswich was really hammered home when I went on a tour of the Emirates Stadium and saw how the Arsenal players are pampered with the very best of everything. They even have individual leather cushions on the dressing room benches to help their circulation and it made me chuckle when I remembered the primitive conditions in our old cricket pavilion in the 50s and 60s. I saw the very latest equipment in the treatment room at the Emirates and recalled my time in the Ipswich equivalent, when a machine equipped with about 30 electric bulbs provided the heat treatment. Players used to occasionally doze off and Jimmy Forsyth would turn up the heat, which usually stopped them overstaying their welcome and quickly got them off the table and back on the training ground.

RAY CRAWFORD
CENTRE-FORWARD 1958–1963 & 1966–1969

BORN   13 July 1936, Portsmouth
SIGNED   1   6 September 1958 from Portsmouth; £5,000
            2   10 March 1966 from West Bromwich Albion; £15,000
IPSWICH CAREER   353 games, 227 goals
HONOURS   Second Division Championship 1960/61, 1967/68; First
Division 1961/62; 2 England caps
LEFT   1   Transferred to Wolves, September 1963; £42,000
           2   Transferred to Charlton, March 1969; £12,000

Ray is the club's all-time leading goalscorer, finishing as top marksman on
seven occasions, and also becoming the first Ipswich player to be capped by,
and score for, England. He netted twice on his debut and hardly stopped
thereafter in his two spells at the club. His fruitful partnership with Ted
Phillips proved the scourge of defences as Alf Ramsey's team swept all before
them to win the Second Division crown and then, in the very next season,
become Champions of England. In his second spell he again helped the club
back to the top flight under manager Bill McGarry and he also went on to play
his part in one of English football's biggest FA Cup shocks, scoring two of
Colchester's goals as they defeated the mighty Leeds United 3-2 at Layer Road
in 1971. His playing days over, he had a spell as youth coach at Portsmouth,
where he still lives.

Ipswich Town 2 v Aston Villa 0

First Division
Saturday 28 April 1962

Portman Road
Attendance 28,932

Ray scores both the goals to clinch a dramatic last-day victory, sparking unprecedented scenes of celebration as it is confirmed that Ipswich really are Champions of England

Teams

Alf Ramsey	**Managers**	Joe Mercer
Roy Bailey	1	Nigel Sims
Larry Carberry	2	Gordon Lee
John Compton	3	Charlie Aitken
Bill Baxter	4	Vic Crowe
Andy Nelson	5	John Sleeuwenhoek
John Elsworthy	6	Alan Deakin
Roy Stephenson	7	Jimmy MacEwan
Doug Moran	8	Alan Baker
Ray Crawford	9	Derek Dougan
Ted Phillips	10	Bobby Thompson
Jimmy Leadbetter	11	Tommy Ewing
Crawford 72, 76	Goals	

Referee: Ernest Crawford (Doncaster)

WE KNEW WE HAD TO win our last game of the season against Aston Villa to have any chance of capturing the League Championship, but we also knew that victory would not necessarily guarantee us the title.

Going into the game we were on top of the table with 54 points and Burnley were two points behind us but with a game in hand and a better goal average. It was clear that if Burnley won their two remaining games, at home to Chelsea on the Saturday and away to Sheffield Wednesday two days later, they would be the champions. Burnley were also just one week away from the FA Cup Final at Wembley, where their opponents were Tottenham, and a great deal was speculated as to whether this might be occupying their thoughts at the same time as trying to bank valuable league points. We had no such concerns and the only thing on our mind was to defeat Villa and hope for the best elsewhere. We went into the game on something of a high, simply because we had such a good win on Easter Monday, five days earlier, when we went to Highbury and played extremely well to beat Arsenal 3-0, with me scoring twice after my pal Ted Phillips put us ahead. On the same day Burnley were held to a 1-1 draw at Blackpool, so whatever happened it was going to be an exciting climax to the season.

The build-up to the game was pretty straightforward and Alf Ramsey, being the shrewd manager he undoubtedly was, didn't work us too hard in training. If we weren't fully fit by then, going into the very last game of the season, there had to be something very wrong. It was just a matter of ticking over for a few days and Alf kept things nice and relaxed around the club. Basically, he was making sure the pressure never got to any of the players. He was good at that and we appreciated him for it, although he had so many other qualities, not just as a manager but as a wonderful human being. His team talk on the Friday was no longer or different to the others he had delivered that season, and he certainly didn't bang on about it being a game we had to win. He talked about Villa and I remember him discussing the threat posed by Derek Dougan, who had been with me at Portsmouth. He was well over the six-foot mark and not dissimilar in style to Peter Crouch, tall and gangly, a real threat in the air but more than useful on the deck due to a good first touch and good awareness. I saw a lot of Crouch when he first played for Pompey and the success he has had since then hasn't surprised me.

I am very pleased to say that our skipper and centre-half, Andy Nelson, looked after big Derek very well that day and that was one of the contributory factors to our win. In all honesty, though, it seemed a pretty low-key game for most of the 90 minutes. I did have an early chance, when Jimmy Leadbetter put me through, but I shot wide. Alf had preached patience beforehand and when we went in at half-time with the game still goalless there was absolutely no sign of panic from him, which didn't surprise us. He just told us to keep passing the ball and I suppose the calm mood in the dressing room was not how a lot of the fans might have imagined it. Alf just told us to relax and the confidence he showed in us made us determined to go out and win the game in the second half, which we duly did. The breakthrough came when we were awarded a free-kick out on the right at the Churchmans end of the ground and Roy Stephenson, who was always a very accurate crosser of the ball, took it. I was quite surprised that Nigel Sims, the Villa keeper, stayed on his line. He was a big lad and I thought he could have claimed the ball, but instead John Elsworthy climbed to power in a header from not much more than six yards out. The ball thudded against the underside of the bar and I instinctively threw myself forward to connect with a diving header and send the ball into the net. I was only a couple of yards out, but it was a classic case of being in the right place at the right time.

The crowd went so wild that it was probably the loudest I had ever heard our fans. It wasn't surprising, given what was at stake, but the game wasn't won yet.

Villa were no slouches, either. They finished seventh that season and their manager, Joe Mercer, had said beforehand that he would insist his players gave nothing less than 100 per cent. They played well, but once they were behind and channelled all their energy into trying to come up with an equaliser, the game opened up and we didn't have to wait long for a second goal. I was being marked by John Sleeuwenhoek and when the ball was cleared by our defence to the half-way line I could feel he had got too close to me, which enabled me to half-turn him and sprint clear. To be fair to him, he had played really well against me and it was about the first time I had managed to shake him off. I had a good start on him and was gone, but when I got close enough to shoot the keeper made a save. He couldn't hold it, however, and it ran loose for me to hit it into the net. At that stage there was only going to be one winner and, if anything, we should have probably had further goals. Both Ted Phillips and Doug Moran had the ball in the net but neither was a goal as the flag went up for offside each time. If the crowd went berserk after the first goal, this time the noise was turned up a few notches and all hell broke loose. There was a buzz among the crowd that it was all-square at Turf Moor but it wasn't confirmed. Nevertheless, when the final whistle sounded, the fans came on to the pitch and were in party mood. Thankfully, within a couple of minutes the news that Burnley had drawn 1-1 with Chelsea was booming out over the PA system and everybody knew we were champions.

Some supporters hoisted Jimmy Leadbetter and I on to their shoulders. Everybody wanted to be part of the celebration, which was fine by me. I always had a close relationship with the fans and I was enjoying the moment. I was just as determined as they were to make the most of an historic occasion. By the time I did get back to the dressing room I was minus my shirt, which had been ripped off my back. I could do nothing to stop it and I often wondered who went home with it and where it is now. I did still have my shorts, socks and boots, but over the years I have parted company with them too. Nowadays, with memorabilia being such a big business, items like that would fetch big money at auctions, but back in 1962 we didn't think like that. In any case, our trainer, Jimmy Forsyth, wouldn't have taken kindly to us either giving away kit or taking it home with us, for the simple reason that the club couldn't afford it and he tended to guard it with his life.

The scene that greeted me once I did get back to the dressing room was one of sheer joy. The famous BBC commentator, Kenneth Wolstenholme, had supplied half a dozen bottles of champagne as a result of a promise made earlier in the season. He was convinced there was no way we could finish above the reigning champions, Tottenham, but he had to cough up. We had enjoyed a major celebration the previous year, when we had won the Second Division, and some other lads had shared Third Division (South) triumphs in the 50s, but this was different. The reality of what we had achieved didn't register at first, but when I stopped and thought about it, the more mind-boggling it became. Alf had performed a miracle – there was no other word for it. It truly was a fairytale how he had taken Ipswich through the leagues, all the way to the very top. We had been favourites for relegation, 100-1 candidates for the title, and we had confounded everyone who had been so quick to write us off. Needless to say, with the champagne flowing, we were all a bit later than usual in getting away from the ground, but that evening I stuck to my usual routine after a Saturday home game of going out in the town with Reg Pickett and our wives.

The club had nothing organised by way of an official celebration, which was perfectly understandable given the fact that the situation at the top of the table was anything but clear-cut as the Aston Villa game approached. We'd have looked a bit daft to be holding a banquet if Burnley had beaten Chelsea and still had a chance of winning the title in their last game at Sheffield Wednesday. What would we have been celebrating? In any case, the club was committed to an end-of-season foreign tour and at 4pm the day after we had beaten Villa we set sail from Harwich on the first leg of a four-game trip to Denmark and Germany. The day after we returned the celebrations started in earnest. A band of Royal Marines led us through the town on an open-top bus to the Cornhill, where we attended a civic reception in the Town Hall. The streets were lined with thousands of fans, who made it a very emotional moment by singing our anthem, Keep Right on to the End of the Road, which was a firm favourite of the players. Three days later we attended another major celebration, a banquet staged by the supporters' club and to which Kenneth Wolstenholme came along. And, typical of Ipswich I suppose, because they never really needed much excuse to have a party, chairman John Cobbold and his fellow directors hosted yet another 'do', this time at the Savoy Hotel in London. I remember travelling up on the train from Portsmouth with Reg Pickett to attend that dinner and the club sent two invitations to all the other Football League clubs, a gesture that went down well.

Once the celebrations ceased and there was time to take stock, it began to dawn on us all what we had achieved. On a personal note, it had been a fantastic season as I was the club's leading scorer with 37 goals in 50 games. Of these, 33 were scored in 41 league games, which enabled me to finish as the First Division's joint top scorer, alongside Derek Kevan of West Bromwich Albion. If you added the 40 I had scored the previous season I had netted 77 goals in 94 games. Plus, I had a League Championship medal, so what was there to be down about? Well, the summer of 1962 coincided with the World Cup finals in Chile and I won't beat about the bush – I thought I deserved to be there. I was playing for the country's top team – there was no point in anyone trying to argue different – and I was also the country's top scorer. I even scored five goals in two games for the Football League. What more could I do to stake my claim? But despite all that, I wasn't named in the provisional squad of 40 that even included some Second Division players.

I did win two England caps that season and there was no prouder player in the land. I provided the pass from which Bobby Charlton scored in the 1-1 Wembley draw with Northern Ireland and I not only kept my place for the next game, against Austria and also at Wembley, but I also scored the opening goal in our 3-1 win. In the summer of 1962 I was 25 and in my prime as a striker, yet it seemed my country didn't want to know. Do I think I got a raw deal from England? Yes, definitely, because I was a goalscoring centre-forward bang in form. Maybe there would be an outcry now from the media if it happened, I don't know. And another thing – my pal Ted Phillips deserved a chance as well. Between us, we scored 61 of Town's 93 goals in our League Championship-winning campaign. Can you imagine the same thing happening now? Me neither. But at least I did manage to play on a couple of occasions for my country and that's something I will always be proud of. I gave away one of my shirts many years ago to a young lad and the other one is on display at Portman Road. Only on loan, I should stress, because I don't want to part company with another one.

YOU KNOW, THERE ARE two things that amaze me about the Ipswich chapters of my career. One, I was dead set against coming to Portman Road in the first place. Two, having been virtually forced into a change of heart when Portsmouth did everything but shove me out of the door and close it behind me, I started to receive poison pen letters from Town supporters who held centre-forward Tom Garneys in high esteem. They made it quite clear that they didn't like the idea of some unknown from Portsmouth trying to replace him and that I would never be as good as him. Tom was a living legend at Portman Road – 143 goals in 273 games by the time he retired in 1959 – but he was 33 and starting to have real problems with his knees at the time I came on board. What the people who wrote the letters didn't know was that the two of us got along very well. In fairness, I also received letters from supporters wishing me well at the club, but I sensed that I never quite won over all my critics and particularly those who made their feelings known in some of the crudest, most basic language I had ever seen in print.

If I'm honest it probably took me the whole of my first season at Ipswich to get Portsmouth out of my system. I was looking for their results every week, while at the same time resenting those who had decided I had no further part to play at Fratton Park. But as I reflect on my time in the game, I thank God that I was wanted by Alf Ramsey. Had that not been the case, where would I have ended up? Who knows, maybe at Gillingham in part-exchange for Ron Saunders when he moved to Pompey? I had good cause to be grateful to Alf, first of all for having sufficient faith in me and then for the expert tuition he delivered throughout our time together. You could say he cast a bit of a spell over me and he had certainly done his homework before paying the £5,000 transfer fee. On my very first day as an Ipswich player he told me about my strengths – scoring goals, running, heading, the fact that I didn't shirk a tackle and that I wasn't afraid to scrap for the ball. Then, almost in the same breath, he rhymed off the areas of my game that I still needed to work on – left foot, positional play, first touch, first-time passing and hold-up play. I couldn't argue because I felt he had summed me up pretty well, but I think he also knew he was buying a player who wanted to learn and improve.

Alf outlined his plans for Ipswich. He wanted to get the club into the First Division within two years and I think he was largely forgiven for the fact that it actually took three. I can't speak highly enough of Alf and I've never heard any of the Ipswich players of that era, or the England team he led to World Cup glory in 1966, say even one bad word about him. He was so modest, so controlled in everything he did, so open, so honest and I never met anyone in all my years in the game who knew more about football than he did. He was also clever in that he knew exactly how to get the best out of each and every one of us. He was an expert in man management. I recall an FA Cup fourth round tie at Stoke in my first season at the club and as we sat in the dressing room just a few minutes away from going out he suddenly said 'I don't think we need to bother playing this game.' That captured our attention and he then produced a copy of the local paper, and started reading from it. The journalist had dismissed our chances and Alf added, more with a smirk than an actual smile, 'Why don't we just get changed and go home?' It served its purpose because we couldn't wait to get out there to prove the writer wrong, which we duly did thanks to the only goal of the game from Derek Rees.

Thursday was Alf's day for his one to ones with players and when it was my turn he would run through what I had done wrong in the previous game and how I should put it right in the next one. I was a bit naïve when I first arrived at the club. It dawned on me that I had not had what I would call proper coaching. Alf helped me a great deal and made me a better player. He took me from nothing and helped to turn me into an England international. Each time I played for England I came back on the train with Alf and he went through the game, saying I should have done this and I should have done that. He said I was doing all Johnny Haynes' running for him. It was always short and sweet, and it never developed into a slanging match. People thought Alf was a bit aloof but he never looked down on people. He also had feelings, even if he didn't always show them. He had come up the hard way, from a poor background, and it was the same with a lot of the players. Alf also had a ruthless streak and I'll never forget how he singled me out after I missed a penalty. 'You'll never take another one for this club' he told me and I didn't. I scored from the spot against Huddersfield in an FA Cup-tie when Ted wasn't playing and I also took our next one in a league game at Bristol City, even though Ted was fit and back in the side. It was pathetic, the poorest penalty you have ever seen in your life, so weak their keeper had to run out two yards to pick the ball up. I couldn't argue with Alf because he was right, as usual.

It's interesting that only one of my goals for Ipswich was a penalty but I admit I was bloody useless at them. Ted was the expert but his main speciality was shooting from distance. I never saw anyone else strike a ball with such power. These days he wouldn't be afraid to shoot from the half-way line, the balls are so light. He has often said I got a lot of my goals from his rebounds and he's right. Keepers regularly spilled his shots and I'd be there to finish it off. I watch games now and that's a dying art. Ted and I hit it off almost straight away and we're still the best of pals, speaking on the phone and seeing each other at the annual reunion, when we are always the last two out the door. We were playing at Plymouth when a long ball down the middle saw their keeper and centre-half collide. I got the loose ball and I could have passed it to Ted but instead I walked it along the goal-line and put it in. 'Greedy bastard,' Ted muttered. I didn't think about passing when I was close to goal. My only thought was to get the ball down and have a shot.

When I was at Wolves the manager, Stan Cullis, said to me one day that he didn't think I scored enough goals from outside the area. I replied that I didn't have a hard enough shot, which was true. Then he turned to Peter Knowles and said 'You don't score enough goals.' Peter thought for a few seconds and said 'No, I cross them for Ray and he scores.' Players were good at specific jobs and my hero was Jimmy Greaves, who I considered to be without equal when it came to putting the ball in the net. You didn't bring Jim back to defend corners – it wasn't his game. When I was with England I remember the manager, Walter Winterbottom, criticising Jimmy's work rate, which I thought was a bit rich. Jimmy scored 44 goals in 57 games for England – there's your answer.

ALF WAS REPLACED AS MANAGER of Ipswich by Jackie Milburn, a lovely man but not cut out to be a manager. He just didn't have it and Town were on the decline when they sold me to Wolves. I was there when Stan Cullis got the sack and was replaced by Andy Beattie, the only Scotsman I have never got on with. I wasn't the only one, thank goodness. I tried to improve team spirit and bonding at Molineux but he was negative about everything I suggested. The Wolves lads would get changed after training and scatter in different directions. At Ipswich we did things together all the time, which had a lot to do with the success we enjoyed. At West Brom the manager was Jimmy Hagan and again he was unpopular with most of the team. Bill McGarry, a real hard man, brought me back to Ipswich and I had a lot of time for him. He treated his players like men and wasn't petty. After Alf, he had the biggest influence on my career and he sorted out the shambles that Ipswich had become. On an away trip to Blackpool I went out with some supporters and missed the curfew. Bill fined me £20. A few weeks later we won at home when Ron Wigg scored twice and I was shit. There's no other word for it, but at least I tried hard. I ran my bollocks off. After the game Bill said 'I've never seen anyone work as hard as you did out there' and handed me my money back.

We won the Second Division title in 1968 but later that year Bill, thinking the grass was greener at Wolves, left us. He talked to me about joining him at Molineux but felt it wouldn't be right for me. I got on well with Bobby Robson, his successor, but there was a problem that we couldn't overcome. In an earlier private conversation, John Cobbold had asked me about my future plans and I told him that I wanted to go to South Africa. Roy Bailey, who was one of my best pals at Ipswich, had gone out there and raved about it. He said he would fix me up with a club, the lot, if I followed him. Mr John said he would arrange a free transfer at the end of the season when my contract was up. I told my wife and she was delighted; it seemed everything was coming together nicely. Mr John said I had earned it for what I had done for the club. But unfortunately Bobby had other ideas because he knew I had value in the transfer market. At that time every penny was being counted and my dream move to South Africa became exactly that – a dream. I moved to Charlton for £12,000 and they doubled my wages to a basic £80 per week. I'd been on £40 at Ipswich, although I also picked up another £20 in appearance money.

The end was in sight when I played for Colchester but my time at Layer Road provided me with one of my career highlights, when I scored twice and we beat Leeds in the fifth round of the FA Cup. I made it to South

Africa eventually and played for Durban City, then I coached at Brighton and Portsmouth, and finally managed Fareham Town, where I succeeded in getting them into the Southern League before the inevitable happened and I was fired. I worked as a merchandiser before I retired. Of all the clubs I played for – and I'm not just saying this for the sake of it – Ipswich were the best. I had my best times there. Mr John was like the head of the family and he created a great atmosphere around the place. With Alf's football knowledge it was a great combination and I feel privileged to have been a part of what I thought then, and still think now, was an absolute fairytale.

KEVIN BEATTIE

DEFENDER 1971–1982

BORN   18 December 1953, Carlisle
SIGNED   July 1971 from apprentice
IPSWICH CAREER 307 games, 32 goals
HONOURS FA Cup 1978; UEFA Cup 1981; Ipswich Player of the Year
1973 and 1974; 9 England caps
LEFT Retired, January 1982

One of British football's all-time greats – according to Sir Bobby Robson, second only to George Best – Kevin's career was tragically cut short by a series of knee injuries that resulted in him failing to fulfil his enormous potential. Such was his impact upon his introduction to the Ipswich side that he became the first-ever winner of the coveted PFA Young Player of the Year award and it was not long before he was being called up to play for his country, adding nine senior caps to the many he had already gained at youth and under-23 international levels. Phenomenally strong, quick and powerful, he formed a formidable central defensive barrier alongside Allan Hunter and also scored some spectacular goals. Despite announcing his retirement, he attempted in vain to make a comeback with both Colchester and Middlesbrough, then after a spell in Scandinavia he returned to Ipswich and was a pub landlord for a time and also enjoyed a stint as an expert summariser on BBC Radio Suffolk. He now devotes his time to caring for his wife, Maggie, who has multiple sclerosis.

Manchester United 1 v Ipswich Town 2

First Division
Saturday 12 August 1972

Old Trafford
Attendance 51,459

Ipswich confirm their rising status with an opening-day victory at a packed Old Trafford as teenage debutant Kevin Beattie upstages George Best and also has a hand in both his side's goals

Teams

Frank O'Farrell	**Managers**	Bobby Robson
Alex Stepney	1	David Best
Tommy O'Neill	2	Mick Mills
Tony Dunne	3	Kevin Beattie
Willie Morgan	4	Ian Collard
Steve James	5	Allan Hunter
Martin Buchan	6	Derek Jefferson
George Best	7	Bryan Hamilton
Brian Kidd	8	Colin Viljoen
Bobby Charlton	9	Rod Belfitt
(Sub. Sammy McIlroy)		
Denis Law	10	Trevor Whymark
Ian Storey-Moore	11	Mick Lambert
		(Sub. Geoff Hammond)
Law 88	Goals	Whymark 8, Hamilton 84

Referee: Eddie Wallace (Crewe)

I CAN THINK OF FEW more daunting places to make your first team debut than Old Trafford, but it is amazing the number of Ipswich players who have done so over the years. It seems I started a bit of a trend because George Burley and Paul Mariner also played their very first games for Ipswich at the same famous venue and, like me, I am sure they will never forget the occasion. One thing I did not have in common with George and Paul, however, is that they both knew they were going to play against Manchester United, whereas I thought I had just been taken along for the ride and genuinely didn't have a clue I was going to be involved at all, never mind from the start.

In fact, I wasn't even paying attention in the dressing room beforehand as the manager, Bobby Robson, ran through the starting line-up. He rhymed off the names of goalkeeper David Best, then skipper Mick Mills and I was next on the list as left-back. But I was sitting there in a daze – I think I was a bit star-struck by the surroundings – and the boss could see I was blissfully unaware that I was playing. "Beat, did you hear me? You are playing," I remember him saying, and it finally sunk in as other players started to congratulate me. My instant reaction was one of panic, but not because I had fears about being able to do myself justice or that I would bottle it.

I had plenty of confidence in my ability, even if the butterflies were fluttering away in my stomach, but the panic was brought on by the fact that I immediately thought of my parents back in Carlisle and how they were going to miss my big day. Needless to say, I had nothing to worry about. When I spoke to the boss he had it all under control. He had let them know I would be playing, but more than that he had given them enough advance warning to ensure they would be in their seats at Old Trafford as I ran out with the rest of the team roughly five minutes ahead of the kick-off.

The boss clearly thought he was doing me a favour by not confirming my involvement until the very last minute. Players are all different and some might need advance warning so as to get used to the idea, while others – and this is the category Bobby Robson clearly felt applied to me – are better hearing the news at such a late stage that they have no time to get nervous and worked up about it. Once the news had sunk in, I was fine about it and when the boss said arrangements had been made on behalf of my parents I just wanted to get out there and get on with it.

Bobby didn't make too much fuss about the fact that it was my debut. I just remember him telling me I was in the side on merit and that he had no doubts about me being able to cope. My direct opponent, United's right-winger, was Willie Morgan, a Scottish international with a big reputation, but Bobby made me feel ten feet tall when he said I would be too good for him. Whether he really felt that I would win my one-to-one with Morgan or not, it was just what I wanted to hear. United were not short of big names at the time, with Bobby Charlton, Denis Law and George Best also in their line-up, and as an 18-year-old who had been playing my football on the council parks in Carlisle just a couple of years earlier it was a moment to cherish.

I made fairly rapid progress at Portman Road but, as I have said, I had no inkling of what lay in store when the boss named me in the party to head north on the Friday. It was the first game of the season and I thought he was simply taking me along to give me a bit of experience, which he did with young players from time to time. I remember the tingle of excitement when the team bus pulled up at Old Trafford but I suppose that was to be expected. From that moment, until the boss named the team, I helped take the team skips into the dressing room and then assisted Cyril Lea with laying out the kit, never even stopping to give it a second thought that I would later be pulling on the yellow number three shirt. When I think back all those years, the boss handled the situation magnificently because I was in a relaxed, but very positive, frame of mind when we were given the signal to make our way out into the tunnel and then on to the pitch.

Crowds were noisier back then, which probably had a lot to do with the way they were packed into the terraces long before the all-seater stadia that are now the norm. The Stretford End was the Old Trafford equivalent of the Kop at Anfield; while they gave their own team a great reception they also did their best to make it an intimidating atmosphere for opposition teams. But if you are going to buckle under the pressure, you are going to be no good to anyone, and the boss had gone out of his way in the dressing room to ensure I was not just going to get by but hopefully thrive in the situation. United regularly play to 76,000 fans these days but, believe me, the 51,000 present 36 years ago really turned up the volume and, needless to say, I had never before experienced anything remotely like it.

I was playing at left-back because Colin Harper, who had played in every one of Town's games the previous season, was suspended. He had been sent off in the home game against Sheffield United, which was the third last game of the 1971/72 campaign, but the suspension did not start until the beginning of the following season and that created a vacancy for the first couple of games that the boss decided I was up to filling. You keep seeing the phrase 'dream debut' and that summed up perfectly my first game for Ipswich, because everything clicked into place virtually from the word go.

Trevor Whymark gave us the lead in the eighth minute and you'll never guess who made the goal for him? I intercepted a pass that was intended for Morgan and set off on a strong overlapping run. Better than that, though, I also delivered the perfect cross from wide on the left that enabled Trevor to open the scoring and we took a firm grip on the game. Without being big-headed, I coped without any trouble and we should have been much further ahead before Bryan Hamilton scored our second goal six minutes from the end, in which I also played a part. Denis Law pulled one back for them with two minutes left on the clock but a lot of the home crowd had already left the stadium by then. The missing fans knew, as we did, that there was no way we were not going to win that game, which we duly did to get our season off to a perfect start.

Okay, perhaps Manchester United were past their best and on the decline – they were certainly not the side who had been crowned European champions just four years earlier – but it was still a tremendous result to go to Old Trafford on the opening day of the season and bring back both points. It was a sign of things to come, in fact, because we went on to finish fourth – the best any Town side had done since Alf Ramsey's team had won the title a decade earlier – and I not only played in 37 of our 42 league games but was also named player of the year in the annual supporters' poll.

But I am jumping a bit ahead of myself. The fine details of what happened during the 90 minutes are a bit sketchy but I do recall that once the final whistle sounded I only had two things on my mind – to meet up with my parents and to collect a few autographs from some of the home players I felt privileged to be rubbing shoulders with. I remember asking Bobby Charlton to sign my match programme and after he obliged he told me 'You're the one whose autograph they are going to be after now.' He was a real gentleman, as I knew he would be from what I'd heard about him, but it didn't sink in at first that I had just played against – and helped to defeat – one of England's all-time greats and the inspiration behind the country's

World Cup success six years earlier. I had watched the win over West Germany in the 1966 final and it seemed strange, not only to be coming off the park alongside the great man but also chatting to him in the players' lounge afterwards.

My parents were in the lounge as well and they couldn't wait to congratulate me. They had been chauffeured down from Carlisle by the club's scout, John Carruthers, and they were having a great time. My old man particularly liked the free bar and sank a few beers before we said our farewells and headed off in opposite directions. It was good to see him and my mum getting on well because I'd been concerned about them for some time. I used to send a bit of cash home to mum and it was intended to help with the household budget. I'm one of nine kids and I knew even a couple of quid would make a big difference. I hit the roof when I heard my dad was not only spending my cash at the pub, which meant others were doing without, but he was also chucking his weight around and my mum was on the receiving end. She had a hard enough time of it without that and I remember going home one weekend to have an old fashioned sort-out with my old man, warning him of the consequences if he ever laid a finger on her again. All that was in the past by the time they saw me at Old Trafford and I was thrilled to make them proud of me.

LIFE AS A PROFESSIONAL footballer with Ipswich could hardly have been any more different to what I had been used to back home. As an athlete the club insisted I ate the best food and my landlady, Mrs Vera Strawn, never let me down. I was able to dress properly, whereas I had arrived in Ipswich a couple of years earlier with the backside hanging out of my trousers and virtually nothing to my name. When you are one of nine kids and your old man has served time – his crime was stealing electricity by rigging the meter in order to keep us warm – life's luxuries tend to pass you by and I lapped up my new life. Instead of being permanently skint, I always had a few bob in my pocket and it was a great feeling to be able to help the four brothers and four sisters I had left behind in our house on the council estate in Botcherby, a typically working class area of Carlisle where it was never too early to learn to look after yourself.

No two ways about it, football changed my life. It opened the door to a lifestyle that was just a dream for anyone with my background. I had a number of jobs when I left school just before turning 15 but I was getting nowhere fast until I attracted the attention of a Liverpool scout and was invited to Anfield for a trial. It went well and I was invited back, at which point I was going to sign for them. I don't think there's anyone who doesn't know what happened next. I travelled down by rail and was expecting someone from the club to meet me. When nobody turned up I switched platforms and jumped on the next train back to Carlisle. Liverpool wrote to me and said I wasn't going to be offered anything after my 'failure to turn up' and I was devastated that my dream seemed to be over. Fortunately, news got round and Ipswich were quickly on the scene and after playing for the youth team at Fulham I was asked to sign on permanently. Back then I was a striker and I scored a barrow load of goals for the youth team before the boss decided to convert me into a defender – and one good enough to play for England.

That first season as a regular member of Ipswich's senior side went unbelievably well and I was the fans' player of the year for 1973/74 as well. I also had the distinction of being chosen as the very first recipient of the Professional Footballers' Association Young Player of the Year award and when I added a call-up to the senior England team I doubt if life could have been any better. I was playing regularly in the centre of defence alongside Allan Hunter by then, the boss having shown enormous faith in me by sanctioning the sale of crowd favourite Derek Jefferson on the basis that I would replace him in the number six shirt. Big Al and I became a formidable double act and I can't thank him enough for all the help and advice he offered throughout our time together.

IT CERTAINLY HASN'T BEEN plain sailing over the years, however, and I'm just grateful that I am still alive to feature in this book after a couple of brushes with death. My career was ended prematurely by injuries to both knees and I am ashamed to say that I almost drank myself to death as well as attempting to take my own life as I hit an all-time low.

I was knocking back the best part of a couple of bottles of vodka a day when I was rushed to hospital with terrible pains after collapsing at home. I had never suffered pain like it; it felt as if I was being stabbed repeatedly. I was in the hospital's intensive care unit and at one stage it looked as if I wasn't going to make it. My wife, Maggie, was called to my bedside one evening and warned to expect the worst. I even had a local priest administer the last rites. But I wasn't ready to go and somehow summoned the strength to fight back. Maybe all that training I was forced to do as a footballer had something to do with it. Despite losing seven stones in weight I managed to walk out of the hospital a few weeks later rather than exit in a coffin as the doctors had at one stage anticipated would be the case.

I was suffering from pancreatitis and there was no doubt my drinking was responsible. I was told in no uncertain terms that another drink could kill me but I have to confess I haven't exactly followed the medical experts' advice over the intervening years. I still like a few beers but my drinking is no longer out of control. Thank God, my suicide attempt also failed, and to say that I feel fortunate to be alive is a massive understatement. I could so easily have said my farewells many years ago but thankfully I was given another chance and even if I lead a very modest existence these days I regard myself as extremely lucky.

My career was packed with many successes and when it was suddenly over I wasn't able to cope. I tried a number of jobs – including, would you believe, pub landlord – but none of them worked out the way I had hoped they would. I had some good times working for BBC Radio Suffolk as a co-commentator, which involved attending Ipswich Town games both home and away, and I also enjoyed contributing a weekly column to the local paper, but again neither role lasted particularly long and for the past few years it has been a case of surviving on benefits. My knees are shot to pieces after years of wear and tear, and I spend most of my time helping to care for my wife, who has multiple sclerosis and is confined to a wheelchair. After being the architect of my own downfall to a large extent, I curse the fact that Maggie has been made to suffer after years of having to put up with me and my apparent death wish.

Apart from the pancreatitis and an attempt to take my own life, when I washed down a bottle of sleeping pills with vodka and was rescued by a friend's knock at the door, I have also suffered a minor stroke. But rather than dwell on the many downs, I prefer to reflect on the high points in a career as a professional sportsman that got under way all those years ago at Old Trafford. The good times far outweighed the bad and the many tributes I have received over the years, particularly from the man I still call boss, have often brought a lump to my throat.

If Bobby Robson thinks the world of me, the feeling is definitely mutual. He has mentioned me in the same breath as Ronaldo – the Brazilian one – and consistently maintained that I am one of the best British players of all time. My only regret is that we didn't have more success to show for our time together at Portman Road, with the absence of a league title a particular bugbear that I know we share. I didn't always toe the line and when I said a few years ago that I felt personally responsible for a number of Mr R's grey hairs I wasn't joking. He always stuck up for me, never gave up on me and dug me out of a few holes of my own making. But apart from a few headaches, I know I gave him no less than 100 per cent commitment when I was out there representing Ipswich, the club I love and will always hold close to my heart.

I will always be grateful to the boss for making my dream come true. I was being well paid for doing something I thoroughly enjoyed but before I knew it my time was up and I only had my memories to keep me going. I should have clocked up another five or six years, but sadly the many cortisone injections I had in my knees took their toll and if I'd continued I'd have been a cripple. As it is, I struggle to climb the steps up to the press box at Portman Road, which is my vantage point these days, and every twinge I suffer is a reminder of what I went through in the pursuit of success.

People really think I am making it up when I tell them I came back within three weeks of a cartilage operation to face Barcelona, who had Johan Cruyff playing for them at the time. But it's absolutely true, as is the fact that I needed three jabs on FA Cup Final day to ensure I not only played against Arsenal at Wembley, but also kept going for the entire 90 minutes. I had one at the team hotel before we set off for the national stadium, another in the dressing room before the game and the third one at half-time. I was in a bit of a state after every game back then – my knee would swell to about three times its normal size – and the cortisone was no long-term cure but simply a short-term solution to enable me to play.

In the end the surgeon left me with no alternative but to call it a day and I don't think I would be human if I didn't look back and think 'What if…' Would shunning the jabs have prolonged my career by a few years? After leaving Ipswich I tried to make a go of it with Middlesbrough and Colchester, also Barnet who were a non-league club then, but I soon realised I was only kidding myself that I could extend my career. Physically, I was just a shadow of the powerfully built player who never shirked a challenge and would fancy himself to outjump and outpace every opponent I came up against. It all came naturally for a while but in the end I was a wreck because there is only so much punishment the human body can take. Wear and tear was one thing, but the booze was another contributory factor and I don't see any point in trying to deny it.

I am just relieved that at least I managed to collect an FA Cup winner's medal in 1978. My defensive partner, Allan Hunter, and I were both rated doubtful until the very last minute and we just about managed to hobble through the 90 minutes at Wembley. We both needed knee operations that summer and it was almost like the beginning of the end for us both. My first team appearances became scarcer each season and it just about summed up my luck that my final game was in an FA Cup semi-final against Manchester City at Villa Park in 1981 when I broke my arm and had to come off. I was thinking in terms of collecting a second winner's medal but it all went pear-shaped on the day, although I didn't realise at the time that I was actually making my farewell appearance.

LIKE I HAVE OFTEN SAID, however, no one can take away my achievements and my happy memories. People say I 'only' played nine times for England and I understand what they mean, as I had to call off on many occasions due to injury. When I was first selected there were a number of people, Bobby Robson amongst them, who expected me to win many more caps. It was even suggested that I would join the select 100 club, but my knees had other ideas. But it still means a great deal to me that I played for England, regardless of how many times it was. I also played for England's youth team in 1972 when we won the Little World Cup, the biggest prize on offer at that level, and there aren't many players who can claim to have done that.

Actually, I came very close to missing that competition because a couple of days before we were due to fly out to Spain I was diagnosed with vaccine fever. Typical of my luck and it got worse because the manager, Gordon Milne, was recommended by the medical people to call up a replacement and leave me at home. When Gordon came to my room in the London hotel where we were staying, and told me of his intentions, I refused to go along with them. I told him 'No way. I will be alright and I won't let you down.' Thank goodness he gave me the benefit of the doubt. Two days later we played our first game and I was in the side, where I stayed all the way through. We beat West Germany in the final in Barcelona and it was one of the proudest moments of my career. Years later, when Gordon was manager of Coventry, he offered £500,000 to buy me from Ipswich but Bobby Robson refused.

I had a testimonial game in March 1982 against Moscow Dynamo and that, along with other events including a sportsmen's dinner, helped to give me a lucrative send-off. As I've often said, however, my attitude to money was always the same – easy come, easy go – and I had no shortage of people who were willing to help me get through the cash. Ultimately, though, I take full responsibility for my actions and accept that I was the architect of my own downfall. I had to sell my house and move into council property, with our latest home converted to enable Maggie to cope as best she can with her disability.

But I'm pleased to say that I haven't completely disappeared off the football radar. As the very first winner of the PFA Young Player accolade, I have been invited back to the annual ceremony and rubbed shoulders with a lot of big-name guests. Also, I was a guest of the Football Association at the first FA Cup Final to be played at the new Wembley in 2007. Before the game there was a parade of Cup-winning legends and it was a real thrill to be invited to represent Ipswich. Furthermore, when the draw was made for the third round of the 2007-2008 competition I was asked, along with ex-Arsenal defender Sammy Nelson, to do the honours. I also have a weekly slot on BBC Radio Suffolk and the phone doesn't stay quiet for too long. If it's not a newspaper man looking for a quote, it's a television company asking me to be a guest on a programme, and with Ipswich being the sort of club they are I am never allowed to forget the glory days of which I was so proud to be a part.

MICK MILLS
FULL-BACK/MIDFIELDER 1966–1982

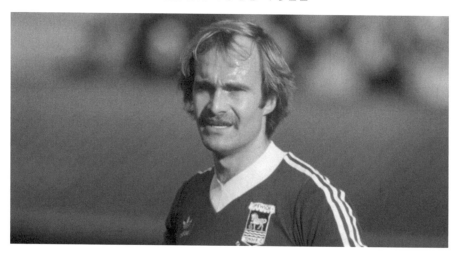

BORN 4 January 1949, Godalming
SIGNED 3 February 1966 from apprentice
IPSWICH CAREER 741 games, 30 goals
HONOURS Division Two Championship 1968; Division One runner-up 1981 & 1982; FA Cup 1978; UEFA Cup 1981; Ipswich Player of the Year 1978; 42 England caps
LEFT Transferred to Southampton, 9 November 1982; £50,000

Only taken on by Ipswich after he was released by Portsmouth, who scrapped their successful youth system for financial reasons, Mick arrived at Ipswich on trial and stayed 17 years, going on to create an all-time appearance record that may never be broken and leading the club to two major honours, the FA Cup and UEFA Cup, in the space of three years. He was also a consistent choice for England and captained his country in the 1982 World Cup finals in Spain. He joined Southampton later that year, helping them to runners-up spot to champions Liverpool in the 1983/84 season, and then went into management with Stoke City, initially as player-boss, before taking charge of Colchester and then assisting ex-Ipswich colleague Terry Butcher at Coventry. He was chief scout at Sheffield Wednesday when Trevor Francis was manager and when Francis took over at Birmingham City he appointed Mick as his number two. Mick, who was awarded the MBE for services to football, is now a partner in Galaxy Sports Management, an agency that represents a number of top footballers across Europe.

Real Madrid 0 v Ipswich Town 0

UEFA Cup first round, second leg
Wednesday 3 October 1973

Bernabeu Stadium
Attendance 80,000

Ipswich are the toast of England – and the talk of Europe – after eliminating the Spanish giants from the UEFA Cup, a tournament they were favourites to win

Teams

Miguel Muñoz	**Managers**	Bobby Robson
Garcia Remon	1	David Best
Jose Luis	2	Mick Mills
Juan Carlos Tourino	3	Colin Harper
Jose Martinez Sanchez Pirri	4	Ian Collard
(Sub. Rafael Maranon)		
Gregorio Benito	5	Allan Hunter
Ignacio Zoco	6	Kevin Beattie
Francisco Aguilar	7	Bryan Hamilton
		(Sub. Peter Morris)
Ramon Moreno Grosso	8	Colin Viljoen
Juan Bautista Planelles Marco	9	David Johnson
Vicente Del Bosque Gonzalez	10	Trevor Whymark
Óscar Tomás Mas Magallán	11	Mick Lambert

Referee: René Vigliani (France)

ONE OF MY MOST VIVID memories of an unforgettable occasion is that immediately after the game I received a bit of a ticking-off from manager Bobby Robson in the Bernabeu Stadium dressing room – but first let me set the scene for you.

With 741 from which to choose it wasn't easy selecting one game above the other 740, but I have plumped for this one because it represented a major landmark in my career with Ipswich and, since it took us to what I would call a different level, was probably even more significant for the club itself.

We had endured several seasons of fighting relegation from the First Division, as the league tables from that era clearly show. Bobby Robson came in January 1969 and we ended that season, our first after winning the Second Division title under Bill McGarry, with a very creditable finish of 12th, which was deemed very satisfactory for a newly-promoted club.

The next two proved more difficult – 18th and 19th respectively – and in 1971-72 we improved to finish 13th. Having started poorly, winning just one of our opening eight fixtures, we finished strongly by only losing one of our last six and it was this run that proved to be something of a launching pad for what followed the next season, when we achieved a far higher level of consistency.

There were a number of reasons for the overall improvement, including the fact that for 12 games on the trot, between November and January, the manager was able to field the same side. We also suffered fewer injuries, which is always a key factor. Bryan Hamilton and I were ever-present, while another two players, Allan Hunter and Trevor Whymark, were only absent once and a further three, David Best, Mick Lambert and Colin Viljoen, were missing just twice. As any manager will confirm, consistency in team selection is a huge plus and we achieved the results to finish fourth, which was brand new territory for all of us and earned us a place in the UEFA Cup for the very first time.

It was a great achievement and, to be honest, entirely unexpected. So much so, that when we were up at HMS Ganges at Shotley, where we spent a lot of our time during pre-season training in those days, the manager called a meeting to discuss bonus payments because qualification for Europe was not even an issue the previous year when the bonus structure for all three domestic competitions had been agreed.

The boss said he had consulted managers like Bill Shankly at Liverpool and Don Revie at Leeds, whose teams were regulars in Europe, for some advice on how to tackle the situation, which seemed a perfectly reasonable approach. By this time the draw had been made, however, and that put a slightly different slant on things. Bobby sat us all down and said 'We need to get this sorted out now' and the players were only too happy to discuss financial matters. In those days the bonuses were important, whereas the current trend is for a higher – very much higher – basic salary.

According to the manager, it was normal throughout the game for European competitions to be treated in much the same way as the two domestic knockout tournaments, the League Cup and the FA Cup. In other words, we would start at a fairly modest figure and the sum would increase depending on our round-by-round progress. That might make sense in some ways but in 1973 we were only on about £20 to win an FA Cup third round tie – the £2,000 bonus we were paid for reaching Wembley in 1978 and the £2,000 extra we received for beating Arsenal and winning the trophy was still a long, long way off.

In any case, we were sure of being involved in the FA Cup third round, but the whole point of the meeting was that we had exceeded expectations by qualifying for the UEFA Cup and having drawn Real Madrid we certainly couldn't guarantee that we would progress to the second round. It meant we had worked the whole season to get into Europe but there seemed every possibility of us receiving very little in the way of a cash bonus for doing so.

That formed the gist of our argument and we made the point that the club would be okay by virtue of the fact that they were sure to have a full house at Portman Road for the first leg, so they would make money. But we wouldn't and we felt that was unfair. We asked for a share of the profits – yours truly, David Johnson, Bryan Hamilton and Colin Viljoen did most of the negotiating on behalf of the entire squad – because that was the only way we could see us being rewarded. Within a few days the manager came back to us and we agreed a 20 per cent share, which we felt was a good deal and with everyone in agreement it meant we could put the matter to bed.

Basically, no-one really expected us to get past Real Madrid and we certainly weren't thinking of going all the way, as we did eight years later, and actually winning it. Looking back, though, I don't think we realised just how good a side we were. In my view the team of 1973 would have given the 1981 UEFA Cup-winning side a game. The draw meant we were at home first, which appeared to give further ammunition to those people who were writing us off as it was generally felt that being away for the opening game provided teams with a better chance of going through to the next stage. It seemed we were really up against it and the general consensus, outside the club, was that our European adventure would be over almost as quickly as it started.

It may be hard to believe now, with television making supporters so much aware of what is going on in the world game, to the extent that we can keep a regular check on what is happening right across the many European leagues, but back in 1973 it was nothing like that. We knew of Real Madrid, of course, because they were arguably the most famous club side in the world, thanks mainly to the fact that they had won the European Cup six times and been runners-up twice before we met them, while I also remembered them from my schooldays and in particular for their 7-3 win over Eintracht Frankfurt in the 1960 European Cup Final played at Hampden Park in Glasgow.

You can imagine how their visit to Ipswich captured the public imagination and there was a terrific atmosphere at Portman Road that night. The Spaniards had their goalkeeper to thank for the fact that they only conceded one goal and I have to confess that I felt a bit disappointed that I was not credited with it. Ian Collard took a short free-kick to me and I cut inside to have a shot, with the slightest of deflections off their defender, Benito Rubinan, taking it into the net.

I have little doubt that if the same incident occurred in a game now – the shot was on target – there would be no argument about who scored the goal. The next day's papers and, more importantly, the club records would show me as the goalscorer. There was another incident that night that didn't seem to make sense either. The referee, Mr Stanislaw Eksztajn of Poland, controversially claimed he had been struck by a missile from the crowd, even suggesting it had been fired from a catapult, and although film of the incident that occurred late in the game clearly showed the official receiving an accidental kick in the calf from Real defender Jose Luis, UEFA still hit Ipswich with a fine imposed in Swiss francs and which was the equivalent of about £685, which may seem like a small sum today but 35 years ago was a substantial amount.

While that was a travesty of justice, nothing could alter the fact that we had beaten Real 1-0, which was a tremendous feather in our cap. I don't think for one minute that they under-estimated us – I believe they were too professional to make that mistake – and by the time we flew to Spain almost a fortnight later for the return leg we were determined that our experience of Europe wasn't going to end at the opening hurdle, even though we were under no illusions as to the difficulty of our task. It had taken us 42 games to qualify through our league position and there was a feeling throughout the team that it would be a real shame if it was all over in two.

From what I can recall we made absolutely no impact upon our arrival at Madrid Airport on the Monday, two days before the game. You hear stories about rival fans waiting to 'greet' teams but there was none of that. I dare say it might have been different for Liverpool and a few other English clubs at certain venues but we had no reputation as far as the Real supporters were concerned and it was all very low-key as we were taken to our hotel.

On the Tuesday we were like a bunch of tourists. Bobby (Robson) loved the European scene and it didn't really surprise me that he went on to devote a large chunk of his career to the continental game in Holland, Portugal and Spain. He really got his teeth into it professionally by going to watch the opposition and whereas managers today can show their players a video or a DVD to highlight certain aspects of the other team's play, he had to rely on painting pictures with his very own words to provide the information he felt we needed to know.

Over the years that we were in Europe he also did his best to conjure up something a bit different for the players. He would do a bit of homework about local history, famous landmarks, that sort of thing, and if there was any suggestion of a lack of interest on our part he wasn't slow to show his displeasure. He felt we should milk the opportunity while it was there for us and if we got the cards out on the bus as we were perhaps having a sight-seeing tour of the host city he would have to make a remark or two, at the same time shaking his head in disbelief. He made no secret of the fact that in his time as a player, and particularly with England, he saw the travelling to foreign parts as a perk of the job to be savoured.

We also had a tour of the stadium and that could have been daunting to some when they saw the trophy cabinet, or room I should say, with all its European Cup replicas and other major honours. We already knew Real were a massive club, but this merely underlined their tradition and the vast amount of success they had enjoyed. Put it this way, we knew what we were taking on but we were not fazed by it.

We trained at the Bernabeu on the Tuesday night and the following morning we had a bit of a work-out, more of a loosening-up session, on what I can only describe as a piece of barren ground not far from our hotel. I doubt if anyone passing by would have believed it if they had been told 'That's the team who are playing Real tonight'.

There was a fantastic buzz about the Bernabeu on the night of the game. In the dressing room beforehand Bobby made sure each player knew as much as possible about his direct opponent and it was a case of giving each of us a 'Do this, do that' type of message. There was much more emphasis on the one-to-ones in those days, whereas now it is more of a collective thing. Bobby would often speak to players individually, sometimes in his hotel room, and we had also had a team meeting, so we had already taken on board quite a lot before the late briefings in the dressing room. He told us to make the most of the opportunity, not to let it pass us by.

I have to say that the Bernabeu is one of the best places I have ever played football. I put it ahead of the Nou Camp at Barcelona, where the crowd do not appear to be on top of you the same. The Bernabeu atmosphere was tremendous and I am very proud of the fact that I never played on the losing side in my three games there. In fact, as a defender, I had a great record – three goalless draws, one with Ipswich and two with England during the 1982 World Cup in Spain, against the host country and one of the very top nations in West Germany, the runners-up that year.

We definitely surprised Real with our approach that night. Their coach admitted later that he fully expected us to sit back and defend, at least for the opening 20 minutes, but we took the game to them right from the start and dominated for long periods. Colin Harper struck the woodwork and we played some high-quality stuff. They didn't expect us to play such an attacking game. We didn't throw caution to the wind, perhaps, but when we were in possession we looked to go forward and tried to score.

Everyone who was around in 1981, when we beat St Etienne 4-1 at their own ground on our way to winning the UEFA Cup, remembers how well we played. It could have been a similar scoreline against Real because there were lots of chances and it would be no exaggeration to say that we could have scored half a dozen goals. It certainly wasn't dull, which you sometimes associate with a 0-0 scoreline, and if we had scored, say, five or six times I am sure people would have talked about it for years. It was a bit like the cake without the icing, I suppose, but it was never a case of them piling on the pressure and us hanging on, as can often be the case. It was exactly the opposite, in fact.

Just as in the first leg, I almost scored. It was in the second half that I lined up a free-kick between the penalty area and the touchline. Real set up a two-man wall, which told me they clearly expected me to play it into the middle for the others to attack, and the position their keeper took up, slightly beyond the middle of the goal towards the far post, only reinforced that view. My confidence was so high – I wouldn't have taken it on if I had been in any way nervous – that I felt I could bend it round the defender to my right and sneak it just inside the near post. That was my intention and it was close, but the keeper managed to scramble along his line and get to it in the nick of time.

AFTERWARDS I HAD TO put up with a fair bit of stick from the other lads. They ribbed me that it was a fluke, a miscued cross, but I knew the truth and that I had come very close to giving us what would have been a sensational win. To be fair, though, we did survive a scare at the other end. I can see it now – the player I was marking, Oscar Mas, managed to get ahead of our defence and had only David Best, our goalkeeper, to beat. But Bestie, who was a bit under-rated even if he could not claim to be top-notch alongside the likes of Peter Shilton and Ray Clemence at the time, pulled off an excellent save to deny him. It would have been really unfair to us if we had lost a late goal and taken the game into extra time because we fully deserved to win, never mind draw, to qualify for the second round.

At the final whistle we acknowledged our supporters, a tiny little pocket of them in among a capacity crowd. We had picked them out beforehand so we knew where they were. We may have had about 10,000 fans in Amsterdam for the UEFA Cup Final against AZ Alkmaar but back in 1973 there wasn't the same scope to head abroad. There were no cheap flights, for a start, so it would have been quite costly for anyone wanting to attend our game against Real and I felt really pleased for those who were present that we had done them proud and made the trip so worthwhile.

Before the two teams disappeared down the tunnel I did something I had never done before while playing for Ipswich – I exchanged shirts with my direct opponent, Oscar Mas. I had just got used to being in the England squad around that time or I probably wouldn't have bothered. It wasn't normal practice the way it is these days, with shirts flying around like confetti, but I was so elated that I couldn't prevent myself and I went into the dressing room clutching the famous white shirt with the number 11 on it.

It was at that point that I received my 'slap on the wrist' from the manager. "Micky," he said, "what have you done?" I didn't have a clue what he was on about, so I replied: "What do you mean, what have I done?" Bobby looked quite concerned and added: "You've ruined the whole set!" That made me realise he was referring to me having swapped shirts and I nonchalantly replied: "Don't worry, I'll buy a new set." I have to confess that immediately I uttered those words I was asking myself 'Why did you say that? It could cost you a right few bob – maybe even more than the bonus for making the next round'. I clocked Bobby again and he was in pensive mood. He used to do that quite a lot, stroke his chin as he considered something. Then he announced: "Go on then, it's a special night, you can all swap shirts if you want to." At that point there was a mass exodus as the rest of the lads made a beeline for the home dressing room.

The pure elation of the achievement, the magnitude of the occasion, was really special. No two ways about it, we were flying. It was our first experience of Europe and we had knocked out the famous Real Madrid. I remember one of the journalists who accompanied us – David Miller, who at that time was working for the Daily Express – made the point that it was not a Real side to compare with the one that featured legends like Ferenc Puskas and Alfredo di Stefano. In those days the media personnel were incorporated within the official party – they were friends of ours and our relationship was vastly different to how it is now – but I recall speaking to David and telling him not to put a dampener on what was still a significant triumph on our part.

Prior to the game, David, who I still see from time to time on my travels, wrote: "Ipswich will go down fighting, for sure. But I fear they will go down." To be fair to him, though, his report afterwards said: "Real were taken apart at the seams and might have finished six down." Jeff Powell of the Daily Mail wrote: "Real, by even the most coldest and most logical of assessments, might have been six down at half-time. So much for our fears that the one goal Ipswich scored in the first leg was nothing like enough to see them through."

The next thing on our minds was to get out and celebrate, so as soon as the coach took us back to the hotel and we had a quick bite to eat, the search was under way to find a bar or a club where we could unwind. It was perfectly normal behaviour. There was no way we could have tolerated being brought to fever pitch, ready for the game of our lives, and then being expected to sidle off to our rooms and go to sleep. To be honest, there was no way that group of players could have been kept indoors that night. We departed with the usual instructions from the manager – "Don't make a nuisance of yourselves, don't hit any waiters, keep an eye on Beattie..." – and it wasn't long before the first drink was being consumed.

I don't want anyone getting the wrong impression here. We were not a hard-drinking bunch. We put the work in and, once the job was done, we just wanted to unwind. Right through to when I left Ipswich in 1982 I cannot remember any group of players that didn't put the work in. The terrific team spirit and camaraderie was a big part of what we had going for us at Portman Road and it didn't just happen. We stuck together as a squad and the club benefited as a result. Some of the lads were friendlier with one or two of their colleagues than others but there were no divisive cliques or Ipswich would never have enjoyed as much success as they did during that era.

No-one had to be dragged out to have a drink, although I'm not denying that some enjoyed it more than others. But it would be exactly the same with any group of young men. You would get some players drifting away after two or three drinks and others would stay on and have another two or three. Don't forget, we had been cooped up in a hotel for most of the previous 48 hours, we had been on a mission and succeeded, and it seemed perfectly natural that we should be looking to unwind together.

WE FLEW HOME ON the Thursday, hit the training ground on the Friday and we were ready to go again on the Saturday, firmly focused on what we had to do. It was a normal routine and we went on to the quarter-final stage of the UEFA Cup that season, only being eliminated by Lokomotive Leipzig after a penalty shoot-out following a 1-1 aggregate draw.

Also, if you check, as I have done, you will see that we did not start the 1973-74 league programme particularly well, winning just three of our opening nine games. But victory over Real was a tremendous fillip and we went on an immediate six-game unbeaten run, eventually finishing fourth in the First Division for the second year in succession, to show we were no one-season wonders, but instead to confirm we were a club growing in status. Indeed, as the record books show, we had a lot more growing to do.

Knowing I was to write about the Real game, I had a bit of fun on the computer to check up on my old mate Oscar Mas. I discovered he had played for Argentina in that controversial World Cup quarter-final against England at Wembley in 1966 – in fact he was an ever-present for his country having also played in all three group games against Spain, West Germany and Switzerland. He scored 10 goals in 37 appearances for Argentina. He only spent that one season with Real Madrid and is best known for being the second highest goalscorer of all time – 199 in 382 games – at the famous River Plate club in Buenos Aires.

I also 'Googled' Vicente Del Bosque, who made his European debut for Real against us at the Bernabeu and was well known as the coach just a few years back. He had a successful time as a player, winning five Spanish titles and two European Cups, and in less than four years in charge of the first team – he was sacked in 2003 – they won two domestic championships and also the Champions League twice. He also succeeded Luis Aragones by taking charge of the victorious Spanish national team that won Euro 2008.

Although I would be the first to acknowledge that in 1973 Real were by no means at their peak, it is clear that they were still a formidable side. German international Gunther Netzer, arguably the best midfielder in Europe at that time, played in the first game at Portman Road and it is interesting that Miguel Muñoz, who was in charge at the time, is still referred to as the most successful coach in the club's history.

TREVOR WHYMARK
STRIKER 1969–1979

BORN 4 May 1950, Burston, Norfolk
SIGNED May 1969, from amateur
IPSWICH CAREER 335 games, 104 goals
HONOURS 1 England cap
LEFT Transferred to Vancouver Whitecaps, February 1979; £100,000

The fact that Trevor never won a major honour in almost a decade at Portman Road cannot conceal his outstanding contribution during that time. Undoubtedly one of the best headers of a ball in the club's history, he was no slouch on the deck either and netted over 100 goals, one of only half a dozen Ipswich players to achieve the feat. Injury denied him an appearance in the FA Cup Final of 1978, by which time the end of his Town career was in sight. Signed after a spell as an amateur, he was one of the players who rose to prominence in Bobby Robson's time as manager. He was the club's top scorer in three seasons out of five in the 70s and is the only Ipswich player to score four goals in a game on three different occasions. He also holds the distinction of scoring the goals that earned Vancouver Whitecaps victory in the North American Soccer Bowl in 1979, after which he played for Sparta Rotterdam, Derby, Grimsby, Southend, Peterborough and Colchester.

Ipswich Town 4 v Lazio 0

UEFA Cup second round, first leg
Wednesday 24 October 1973

Portman Road
Attendance 26,433

Ipswich establish a handsome lead against a side only narrowly pipped for the Serie A title the previous season and who would go on to become Italian champions in the 1973/74 campaign

Teams

Bobby Robson	**Managers**	Tommaso Maestrelli
David Best	1	Felice Pulici
Mick Mills	2	Mario Facco
Colin Harper	3	Luigi Martini
Peter Morris	4	Giuseppe Wilson
Allan Hunter	5	Giancarlo Oddi
Kevin Beattie	6	Franco Nanni
(Sub. Geoff Hammond)		(Sub. Pierpaolo Manservisi)
Bryan Hamilton	7	Renzo Garlaschelli
		(Sub. Vincenzo D'Amico)
Colin Viljoen	8	Luciano Re Cecconi
David Johnson	9	Giorgio Chinaglia
(Sub. Clive Woods)		
Trevor Whymark	10	Mario Frustalupi
Mick Lambert	11	Sergio Petrelli

Whymark 17, 43 47, 62	Goals	

Referee: Bertil Loow (Sweden)

NO STRIKER COULD POSSIBLY forget scoring four goals in one game and in my case, doing it in a European tie, against a very defence-minded Italian side determined to keep things tight away from home, it was a moment to cherish, which is why I have chosen this particular game. But when I think back to the events of that memorable night in 1973, I can recall far more than the game itself. I also remember a pretty remarkable sequence of events leading up to the game and not being in a particularly good mood for most of the day after we had a training session on the Portman Road practice pitch in the morning. It was nothing too strenuous, for obvious reasons, and it was more of a loosening up session, with a few practices on various free-kicks thrown in for good measure.

Most of the players were a bit surprised when the manager said we would finish with some functional play. The first one broke down with one member of the squad – I honestly cannot remember who – and out of pure frustration he booted the ball away. We started again and this time it broke down with me, which prompted me to whack the ball as hard as I could and it sailed off into the distance.

"Go and get the ball, please, Trevor," said the boss, to which I acted very surprised and not a little bit annoyed. I didn't like the fact that he was singling me out and trying to belittle me in front of my colleagues. As I started to show my displeasure, he simply repeated the same "Go and get the ball please," message, which wound me up even more. However, despite my anger, I set off to retrieve the ball and as soon as I returned the manager announced, "Right, that's it, end of the session, everybody in."

I was a little bit upset, to say the least, and as I joined the other players in walking off towards the dressing rooms I heard the manager's voice calling my name. You can probably guess how I felt. 'What is it now?' I was thinking to myself as I stopped, turned round and started to make my way back towards him. As I reached him, the manager said 'Tonight, I want you to play in a role you have never played in before.' He went on to explain that he and his backroom staff had watched Lazio and noted that they not only played with a sweeper, Giuseppe Wilson, but that he apparently preferred to play deeper than most, particularly away from home. The manager then went on to outline what was expected of me in what he stressed was an unfamiliar role.

He said I would be man-marked for certain and asked me to push as far on to the sweeper, Wilson, as I could. If I did that, he explained, it would leave my strike partner, David Johnson, one on one with his own marker, who was not the quickest of players. The manager said the plan would enable Jonty, who was extremely quick, to exploit the situation. It was clear a great deal of thought had gone into the preparations. Basically, the manager and his staff had it all worked out the way the game was likely to go and he made it abundantly clear to me that he envisaged Jonty's pace – together, obviously, with his eye for goal – would be our best bet in terms of establishing a first leg lead.

I listened to what he had to say, nodded and said I understood, and I thought that was the end of the conversation. As I turned and walked away, though, I again heard his voice calling my name. I turned round to face him and he said 'Bit petulant, earlier, I thought.' Before I had a chance to think of a reply he spoke again, this time to say 'But that might be the only kick of a ball you get today, because of the way I have asked you to play tonight.' It was clear he had nothing else to say, so I turned on my heels and headed back to the dressing room, feeling even more aggrieved at how I had been treated. I wasn't an inexperienced apprentice who had to be taught a lesson, I was an experienced professional, and I most certainly did not think the put-down was either necessary or appropriate.

I was still fuming after I had showered and changed, and also as I got into my car for the journey home. I was living in Onehouse, near Stowmarket, at the time and for the entire trip I kept mulling the situation over in my head, always arriving at the same conclusion, that he didn't have to make so much of it and embarrass me in front of the other players the way he did. Because it was a match day, the training had finished early and my normal routine would have been to get home and unwind, maybe even take myself off to bed for an afternoon kip. But I was so wound-up inside that I instead carried on with something I had started the previous weekend, decorating the hallway of our house. I not only painted it, but also wallpapered it, and I must have spent about two and a half hours doing it, after which I was pretty tired, although my anger at what had happened earlier had far from subsided.

Back then we didn't have team meetings and pre-match meals at the Centre Spot, which later became the norm under Bobby Robson. The players ate at home, usually a light meal like poached eggs on toast, and then reported to the ground about an hour before the kick-off. But when I was getting towards the end of my wallpapering stint, and my wife Rita asked me what I wanted to eat, I remember telling her 'I fancy toad in the hole, roast potatoes and all the trimmings.' She duly cooked it and I ate the lot. After that it was time to get ready and the club operated a strict dress code that required the players to wear shirt and tie. But instead of putting on a suit I chose some corduroy jeans and an open-neck shirt, making sure I did not wear a tie nor take one with me. When I arrived at the ground, I parked under the gymnasium and made my way to the dressing room via the tunnel that led out on to the pitch.

I was at one end of the corridor that passed both the home and away dressing rooms, but there was another door at the opposite end, close to the club's ticket office and reception area. I remember thinking 'What if the manager just happens to walk through as I'm on way to the dressing room and spots that I'm not smartly dressed?' It could have meant a club fine, so it was important, but in the end I decided to take a chance and sprinted up the corridor and into the dressing room before anyone spotted me. I duly whipped off my gear, changed into my kit and sat on the bench, so neither the manager or the first team coach, Cyril Lea, were any wiser as to what I was wearing when I arrived at the club.

I should probably make it clear that I was no trouble-maker at the club. That was the one and only time in my 10 years at Portman Road that I reacted the way I did. Maybe, given the eventual outcome, I should have rebelled more often. But you are what you are – in my playing days I was the type who didn't react with an outburst but preferred to keep things bottled up inside me. With about five minutes to go until we left the dressing room the manager said 'Trevor, do you know what you are doing? Are you sure you know what I expect from you?' At the time I remember wondering why he had sprung it on me so late and also why we had not worked on it at all in training. He also repeated the same instructions he would dish out before just about every game I played for Ipswich. There were four things he would drum into me – 'Chase the full-back, hold the ball up, don't flick it off, come back with the centre-half at corners.' From time to time he tried to catch me out by saying them in a different order. He said not to flick the ball off, but what he meant was that I had to know whether it was best to hold the ball up or flick it on, which led to quite a few goals over the years.

THE WAY WE PLAYED back then wasn't dissimilar to how Wimbledon played a few years later, but we had the subtlety they perhaps lacked. We used to play it into the front men from the back four, bypassing the midfield, and the midfield lads would be looking for the ball to be laid back to them. It took me only 17 minutes to score my first goal against Lazio and I suppose it was the type of goal that supporters who were around in the 70s would most associate with me. Mick Lambert sent over a right-foot cross for me to rise and head into the net.

Our second goal came just before half-time and again it came from a left-wing centre. This time it was Colin Harper who crossed low into the box and I actually mishit the ball. Sometimes you hit the sweetest of shots and the keeper makes a wonderful save, but on this occasion I hit the ball into the ground with my left foot and because he was anticipating a much better effort it simply bounced over him. Just two minutes after the break I completed my hat-trick and again it was created down the left side as Colin and Mick combined, leaving me to score from just inside the six-yard box. Just past the hour mark I netted my fourth, when Colin Viljoen's shot hit me on the back and the ball dropped nicely for me to hit a low shot with my right foot. The Lazio players protested that the ball had come off my hand but the referee was having none of it.

About five minutes from the end I actually missed the easiest of the five chances that came my way on the night. I closed in on the keeper and maybe because I was feeling confident, having already scored four times, I decided to have a go and the ball flew wide. Needless to say, of course, it was a very happy dressing room because a 4-0 win was beyond our wildest dreams, particularly as Italian teams had a reputation for being ultra-defensive away from home. The game had certainly not panned out the way the manager and his coaches had perhaps envisaged it would and I think he was totally oblivious to the fact that earlier in the day I had been thoroughly pissed off with him and the way he had treated me. Amidst the celebrations we all felt for David Johnson, who picked up a horrendous injury that forced him to come off. We hadn't realised just how bad it was at the time and only learned the full extent of the damage afterwards.

Maybe the most surprising aspect of my four-goal display against Lazio, which earned me an award from Roma supporters when we flew to Italy for the return game, was that only one of the goals, the first, was a header. I have no idea how many of my 104 goals for Ipswich were headers, but I would guess about half of them. My ability in the air was down to years of practice as a youngster. My dad played amateur football for Diss and Norfolk, and although he earned himself a trial at Norwich he suffered from cartilage trouble and never made the professional ranks. He passed on a lot of advice and was always encouraging me. I used to practice my heading against a wall of the house for hours on end and it must have seemed like an eternity to our next-door neighbour. The poor bloke worked nights so he would get home and was trying to sleep as I started to practice the minute I got back from school. I had one of those Frido plastic balls that all the kids had at the time.

IPSWICH SPOTTED ME PLAYING for Norfolk against Suffolk at youth level and in those days I was a right-winger. I wasn't very tall – my nickname at school was Half Pint – and to be honest I didn't realise what a great opportunity it was to be playing regularly in the youth team. Our games would kick off at about 11am on a Saturday and I would make a quick getaway and hitch a lift home before heading over to Diss Town's ground to play for them. Laurie Sivell was the youth team keeper and I owe at least some of my success to him. He was left-footed and his goal-kicks would usually come over to our right flank, where I would get across the opposition left-back and head the ball on. One day the chief scout, Reg Tyrell, came to me and said they were thinking of trying me as a striker and that was how it all came about. The season ended a few weeks later and I received a letter from the club in the summer, complete with signing-on forms, asking me to continue in the new season. I had a growth spurt over 18 months or so and shot up to 5ft 10ins.

But there was one problem that arose, which caused some confusion and embarrassment. I was in the pub in Diss one night when a chap said 'You didn't score today then?' I said that I had got a goal and he drew my attention to a report in the local paper that identified the scorer as Trevor Walsh. At our next game Reg called me over and owned up that he was playing me despite the fact that I was too old. The rules stated that I had to be under 18 on September 1, yet my 18th birthday had been in May. Reg's 'solution' was to call me Trevor Walsh on the forms but he then went on to explain that one of the supporters who watched youth team games and knew my surname was Whymark had asked him why I was down as Walsh on the team sheet. Reg then floored me when he added 'To cover myself I've told him that your mother and father got divorced, your mother remarried and you have taken the surname of your stepfather. Is that okay?'

I felt I had no alternative but to go along with it – all I wanted was to continue playing – but the problem resurfaced a few months later when we had a change of manager and Bobby Robson was appointed. The new boss had obviously been looking at what he had at his disposal and found the discrepancy, at which point I was dragged into his office. He told me I was too old to be playing in the youth team and I innocently replied 'Yes, I know, but I was unaware of that until Mr Tyrell told me.' The manager was adamant and said 'You can't do that. Let me speak to the other coaches and I will get back to you.' Soon afterwards I received a letter inviting me to have a month-long trial and, since I was too old for the youths, I was told I would be playing in the reserve team. Naturally, I accepted and upon arriving at Portman Road I bumped into Reg, who had a right go at me. 'Why did you tell Robson? I'm in all sorts of bother now,' he said, but as far as I was concerned I was the innocent party and had done nothing wrong, unless you count being born a few months too early.

I thought that was the end of the matter until I was asked to go and see the secretary, Wally Gray, who told me 'We will be continuing to pay your travel expenses, but we won't be paying for you to travel First Class any more.' I said nothing but I realised what had been going on. Reg used to pay me the equivalent of the Second Class rail fare every week, but he was clearly collecting the First Class fare from the club and pocketing the difference. I had nothing to complain about, however, because I very rarely bought a ticket. I discovered that if I got on the train at Diss without buying a ticket I could then slip through the parcels office at Ipswich without anyone knowing. The fiddle became even more elaborate when Clive Woods came on the scene because he would already be on the train from Norwich when I got on at Diss. He travelled with his uncle, who happened to work for British Rail and was entitled to free travel. When the ticket collector came along Clive and I used to pretend to be asleep and his uncle, who knew the collector, said we were with him, which meant that neither of us had to pay.

Ipswich seemed to be in no real hurry to sign me because my month's trial actually lasted three months and I didn't sign my first professional contract until my 19th birthday. Clive also signed as a pro on the very same day and we consolidated our places in the reserves. He managed his senior debut a few months ahead of me, and while I went on to make 335 first team appearances, he clocked up 338, so there wasn't a great deal of difference in our careers. Back in the early days of Bobby Robson's reign, Ipswich were struggling to survive in the top flight and in my view one of his best decisions came towards the end of the 1969/70 season, when we were embroiled in a desperate relegation battle. We had about eight games left to play and he called a meeting with the 17 players he said would get us out of trouble. It was a decisive move and it lifted morale among the group. It was good to know he had sufficient belief in me and we duly scraped clear of trouble.

In the early days it wasn't plain sailing for me at Ipswich – in fact, anything but. I was among a group of young players that also included Woodsy, Mick Lambert, Roger Osborne, Johnny Miller and Geoff Hammond, and we were given a pretty tough time of it. We were constantly being taunted by the manager saying things like 'Who signed you? You should be sweeping the streets or cleaning toilets.' It was almost as if he was operating a rota because we seemed to take turns at being on the receiving end. Roger, in particular, was regularly slaughtered and it was poetic justice, in a way, that his career should reach such an amazing high when he scored the winning goal in the FA Cup Final.

I am certain the manager would say that he was using reverse psychology and only wanted to gee us up so that we would realise our potential, but I'm afraid I didn't see it that way. Different players need different types of motivation; while some responded to what I thought bordered on bully-boy tactics, there was also a risk that others who had just as much, or maybe even more, talent might fall by the wayside. I have only met Sir Bobby once since I finished playing and what's done is done as far as I am concerned – water under the bridge, you might say. I have tremendous respect for what he has achieved and how he has gone about it, but I have other opinions that I would prefer to keep to myself.

I remember one particular day when I was feeling extremely low because the manager had a go about something I considered to be quite trivial. I was trudging off the practice pitch when Ray Crawford came up and put his arm round me. Ray was in his second spell with the club and there was nothing anyone could teach him about playing up front. He encouraged me to keep doing the things I was good at and to reach a level of confidence where the other aspects of my game would automatically improve. It was very useful advice and I was glad to have the opportunity of speaking to someone like Ray, because fairly soon after that he moved on to Colchester and, I'm pleased to say, my career did eventually take off.

The obvious personal low was missing the FA Cup Final in 1978. I had suffered a serious knee injury in the East Anglian derby against Norwich at Carrow Road, on Boxing Day 1977, and the final came along too soon for me. I did recover to play three league games, scoring in two, including the one we lost 6-1 at Aston Villa a week before the final, but I was well below the level of fitness I would have needed to play at Wembley. It was painful at the time, just as it has been when the various anniversaries have come round, but there's nothing I can do to alter the fact that, sadly, I missed out on what for most footballers is a once-in-a-lifetime opportunity. I didn't make any sort of contribution towards our FA Cup success and for that reason I didn't attend the 30th anniversary reunion in 2008 – I just didn't feel I belonged there. I was mulling it over until I saw the itinerary and the open-top bus ride was enough to put me off.

While I missed out at Wembley, though, I did manage to win an England cap, something I am extremely proud of, given my humble start in the game. I scored three goals in seven under-23 games and I was one of five Ipswich players, along with Kevin Beattie, Brian Talbot, Paul Mariner and Woodsy, who were included in the senior squad for a World Cup qualifier in Luxembourg in October 1977. Ron Greenwood was the manager who picked me and I think he rated me as a player because he was the only club boss, when he was in charge of West Ham, who made a habit of coming up to me after games to shake my hand and say 'Well done.' PM started the game while I went on for Terry McDermott and Beat replaced Dave Watson in our 2-0 win. Brian was an unused sub and Woodsy, unfortunately, didn't make the bench.

I LEFT IPSWICH TO JOIN Vancouver Whitecaps in the North American Soccer League and from a playing point of view it was a tremendous experience. One of the highlights for me was lining up alongside a truly great player in Alan Ball. Even if it was towards the end of his career, the things he did made you realise how good a player you had to be to appear in the same team. I also played against some of the all-time greats, including Johan Cruyff and Franz Beckenbauer, as well as several of the Brazil and Argentina players from the 1978 World Cup. The travelling was a pain, however. Away trips sometimes took three days and often saw us passing through four different time zones. Because we were in Canada it wasn't always possible to get direct flights and we often found ourselves hanging round airports for several hours waiting for a connection. Making the long journeys by road from Ipswich was bad enough, but this was something else.

From a football perspective, however, it was extremely worthwhile and I was fortunate to score the two goals when we defeated Tampa Bay

Rowdies 2-1 in the Soccer Bowl. We beat the New York Cosmos over two games in the semi-final and the away leg pulled in an 80,000 full house at the stadium adjacent to Flushing Meadow, where the US Open tennis takes place. Because Cosmos didn't make the final, it attracted only 55,000 fans. It was Rodney Marsh's farewell game for the Rowdies and my team-mates included ex-Wolves keeper Phil Parkes, former Scotland winger Willie Johnston and ex-Fulham midfielder Ray Lewington, while my strike partner was Kevin Hector, who helped Derby to win the League Championship and also played for England. Vancouver is a wonderful city and we were one of the best supported clubs in the NASL, regularly pulling in between 25,000 and 30,000 fans. But soccer wasn't that popular everywhere else and there were a few occasions when we would play in a baseball or American football stadium in front of just 2,000 fans and the atmosphere wasn't much better than in a Sunday morning league game.

While I was in Canada I arranged a loan transfer to Norwich. Their manager, John Bond, and his assistant, Ken Brown, came out to see me play and negotiate a deal with me and the club. But before I left Vancouver, manager Tony Waiters told me the deal was off because the Football Association were insisting that I could not return for the start of the NASL season in March and I would have to stay until the English season finished the following month. I had a short spell in Holland with Sparta Rotterdam but I didn't enjoy it and moved on to Derby, where I was struck down with glandular fever after two games and soon after that it was time to head back across the Atlantic for my second season. Once that was over, I joined Grimsby as player-coach, only to be injured – at Portman Road of all places – within two minutes of the start of an FA Cup fourth round tie in January 1983.

My next club was Southend, after which I retired, but within a few days I had a phone call from John Wile, the Peterborough manager, who was short of strikers. I wasn't there long and then I heard from my former Ipswich coach, Cyril Lea, who was the Colchester manager. He asked me to help him out after a striker was injured and I was at Layer Road for about six weeks before I finally called it a day. I did six years' coaching at both the Ipswich and Norwich academies but while I thoroughly enjoyed the work it was difficult to fit it in around my full-time job as a salesman/driver.

ALLAN HUNTER
CENTRAL DEFENDER 1971–1982

BORN   30 June 1946, Sion Mills
SIGNED   9 September 1971, from Blackburn Rovers, £70,000
IPSWICH CAREER   355 games, 10 goals
HONOURS   FA Cup winner 1978; Ipswich Player of the Year 1976; 53 Northern Ireland caps
LEFT   Released April 1982, appointed player-manager of Colchester United

Few players in the history of Ipswich Town FC enjoyed cult status to the same extent as Allan in his 11 years at Portman Road. Not only was he an old fashioned centre-half, who defended as if his life depended upon it, he was also a jovial, fun-loving character with whom the supporters identified and took to their hearts. His partnership with Kevin Beattie was the rock on which Town's success in the 70s was built and he was an inspiration to his colleagues just by his presence in the side. Wholehearted, committed, uncompromising . . . he was all of these, but what set Allan apart was that he was on the same wavelength as the fans with whom he enjoyed such a strong rapport. The club's most capped international, all but six of his Northern Ireland caps were won during his time as an Ipswich player. After a brief spell as manager of Colchester United he worked at Felixstowe Docks before returning to Layer Road as first team coach under Mike Walker, only to lose his job when Walker was dismissed in 1987. Now retired, he spent more than 20 years working with people with learning disabilities, putting to good use his skills as a carpenter, having served his apprenticeship before coming to England.

Lazio 4 v Ipswich Town 2

UEFA Cup second round, second leg
Wednesday 7 November 1973

Olympic Stadium, Rome
Attendance 20,000

Ipswich do enough to qualify for the next round but are on the receiving end of unprecedented violence as their players come under attack during and after a tempestuous clash

Teams

Tommaso Maestrelli	**Managers**	Bobby Robson
Felice Pulici	1	David Best
Mario Facco	2	Mick Mills
Luigi Martini	3	Colin Harper
		(Sub. Geoff Hammond)
Giuseppe Wilson	4	Peter Morris
Giancarlo Oddi	5	Allan Hunter
Franco Nanni	6	Kevin Beattie
Renzo Garlaschelli	7	Bryan Hamilton
Luciano Re Cecconi	8	Colin Viljoen
Giorgio Chinaglia	9	Clive Woods
		(David Johnson)
Mario Frustalupi	10	Trevor Whymark
Vincenzo D'Amico	11	Johnny Miller
(Sub. Sergio Petrelli)		
Garlaschelli 1, Chinaglia 28, 85 pen, 88 pen	Goals	Viljoen 73 pen, Johnson 89

Referee: Leo van der Kroft (Holland)

LET ME MAKE ONE thing absolutely clear – my choice of this game ahead of the many others I played for Ipswich has absolutely nothing to do with football. If I was selecting the game in which I possibly played better than in any other I could have gone for the FA Cup semi-final when we beat West Bromwich Albion at Highbury in 1978. It was a marvellous occasion and I know I played well. Yes, I gave away a penalty, something I'm not likely to forget, when I handled the ball from a cross at a time when we were 2-0 ahead. Why did I do it? I haven't a clue – I honestly can't explain it. But all that mattered that day was that we won and we were through to the final. Just after he blew the final whistle, referee Clive Thomas came up to me and said 'You had a tremendous game today' and shook my hand, which I thought was a terrific gesture.

Another game that has stuck in my mind took place in my very first season as an Ipswich player. It was the final home game, played on a Tuesday night, and we beat Manchester City 2-1, a result that cost them the league title. I was quite friendly with City winger Mike Summerbee and he came up to me at the end and said 'Have you lot been got at?' I said I hadn't a clue what he was talking about and he replied 'Were you paid money to beat us?' Mike was actually suggesting we might have been bribed by a rival manager – I'm not saying who – which was nonsense, but he couldn't figure out how we had beaten City when we had nothing to play for. It was straightforward – we were the better team on the night, simple as that.

Real Madrid away in the UEFA Cup was another special game as far as I am concerned. Because we had a slim, one-goal lead from the first game at Portman Road, I think the Spaniards expected us to defend in depth and try to hang on to it. When we went out and took the game to them, which was the very opposite of what they were anticipating, they struggled to cope and we might have had as many as half a dozen goals that night. But Mick Mills has beaten me to it in plumping for the goalless draw at the Bernabeu Stadium so I've gone for another European tie from the same UEFA Cup campaign – and one that is memorable for all the wrong reasons.

I would be lying if I said I expected the second leg of our second round tie to be incident-free. We – or should I say Trevor Whymark, who scored all our goals – had given Lazio a real pasting at Portman Road. They were lucky to escape with a 4-0 defeat and they knew it. But it was clear they were hurt and quite possibly, as they licked their wounds and made their way home, they were already plotting their revenge by whatever means possible. They didn't like it one bit and it showed. There were one or two incidents that night, mainly the terrible injury that David Johnson sustained, which suggested the game in Rome would be anything but plain sailing. Poor old Jonty was kicked in the unmentionables and we had no doubt it was intentional. He was patched up with several stitches and the spring in his step was missing for several days.

There's a famous story about Jonty being down at Portman Road a couple of days later while a board meeting was in session. Our chairman at the time, John Cobbold, saw him and asked how he was. That was Jonty's cue to drop his trousers and let the directors see for themselves. Only he went a step further and plopped his you-know-what on the boardroom table, at which point the directors winced and one of them said 'That's terrible, it looks as if you need a transplant'. Jonty replied 'Not from any of you buggers, thank you very much' as everyone burst out laughing. It was typical Ipswich – we were not known as a fun club for nothing – and although Jonty still wasn't anywhere near 100 per cent fit by the time we flew to Rome for the second game, he was adamant he was up to being on the bench, which was just as well as things turned out.

Despite their obvious hurt at being walloped at Portman Road, none of us bargained for what the Lazio players had planned for us in the return game and I can honestly say that I have never witnessed anything remotely as bad as what we encountered in the Olympic Stadium. Even now, 35 years on, I can scarcely believe what occurred that night. It was an absolute disgrace, something that I wouldn't have thought possible unless I was there to witness it with my own eyes. Lazio plumbed the depths with their outrageous behaviour, but more of that later.

There was not even the slightest hint of what was to follow as we arrived at the airport in Rome on the Monday, two days ahead of the game. There was no hostile reception and it was all very calm as we made our way to the coach that was waiting to transport us to our hotel. Incredibly, given the treatment their players meted out little more than 48 hours later, the club could not have been more hospitable and even provided us with exclusive use of their team bus for the duration of our stay. Very nice it was, too.

The one unusual incident that did occur prior to the game was that a group of Roma supporters visited our hotel and sought out Trevor to present him with a special award for his four-goal display in the first game. Pictures were taken and they appeared in the local newspapers on the day of the match, which probably did nothing to discourage the Lazio players and supporters from waging war on their Ipswich counterparts. Look at it this way – imagine if the same thing occurred in Manchester, Liverpool or Glasgow. Of course it would be like a red rag to a bull, although that in no way excuses what we had to endure.

We were in Rome on serious business but Bobby Robson was the type of manager who encouraged the players to relax and enjoy the experience of competing in Europe. Don't forget, it was all new to us in those days. We had been to Madrid the previous month and done the sightseeing bit, and there was even more to see in Rome. So we saw all the famous landmarks, had a look round some like the Colosseum, between training, and going into the game we were in good shape. With a four-goal lead, we were also confident of going through, little realising that we were about to go to war to protect it and that we were in for an experience none of us would ever forget. Mick Lambert was ruled out with a foot injury he had picked up in our previous game at Coventry four days earlier. The decision was not taken until very late – the manager wanted to give him as long as possible to recover – and so Johnny Miller made what was to prove his only European start for the club.

Bobby Robson told us beforehand that it could turn ugly. This was based on a conversation between him and Bertie Mee, the Arsenal manager at the time. Bertie had rung Bobby and spoken to him about what happened to his team a couple of years earlier. He warned Bobby that the players would kick us, spit in our faces and do anything possible to try to swing the tie in their favour. There had been trouble at the stadium when Lazio played Arsenal, then players of both sides clashed after an official dinner in a city centre restaurant. The fighting spilled into the street and the upshot was that Lazio were banned from Europe for two years but, as we were about to discover, they had not learned their lesson.

Bobby stressed the need for us to show plenty of discipline and not get involved. Lazio's reputation went before them but they were also regarded as a good team, having finished third in Serie A the previous season, which earned them a UEFA Cup place for the very first time. The fact that they were Italian champions in 1974 – their first such honour – showed they were no mugs, except of course they were unable to compete in the

European Cup because of the ban imposed on them for their behaviour during and after the game against us.

When you are playing in Europe, especially away from home and you are defending a first leg lead, the last thing you want is to concede an early goal. That's exactly what we did, however. A total of 43 seconds had expired when the ball rebounded off my knee and one of their players sent a shot past David Best, just inside the post. Giorgi Chinaglia, their centre-forward, was someone who had grown up in Wales and been given a free transfer by Swansea, only to get his career back on track with Lazio. Within a few minutes he tried his luck with an overhead kick and it struck the top of the crossbar, then a bit later on I had to make two goal-line clearances to prevent him from scoring. One of the clearances led to claims for a penalty as the Lazio players accused me of handling the ball, which was definitely not the case.

It was Chinaglia who put Lazio further ahead and there was no sign of the pressure receding as they kept going at full pelt. Off the park, we were aware of trouble on the terraces as our small pocket of fans was attacked by home supporters. The temperature inside the stadium was rising all the time and the best thing that could have happened was for us to score. When their keeper dropped a long-distance shot from Peter Morris, the first player to reach the loose ball was Clive Woods but unfortunately his effort hit the post. We had more bad luck when Colin Harper went down injured near the touchline and to be fair it looked an innocent challenge. He was unable to continue and while he recovered to play further games for the club, the knee injury he picked up in Rome was what led to him having to retire prematurely.

It was still 2-0 to Lazio at half-time and I have to confess I feared the worst. We were really under the cosh and if Lazio were going to maintain a similar tempo for another 45 minutes we would be doing well to hold out. Ironically, it was their thuggery that proved to be the undoing of them. They clearly believed their best bet of achieving the result they needed to qualify for the third round was to quite literally kick us off the park, as well as spitting in our faces in an effort to intimidate us. One of the first signs of this was when Chinaglia followed through on goalkeeper David Best, who needed treatment to his thigh before being able to continue. But although Lazio were doing all they could to unsettle us we kept on playing and it needed excellent saves from their keeper to keep out efforts by Peter Morris and Clive Woods.

With almost half an hour of the second half gone we were awarded a penalty when Woodsy was tripped. The ref was brave enough to give it but the second he blew his whistle and pointed to the spot all hell let loose. The Lazio players protested that Woodsy had dived and I even saw a linesman being head-butted by one of them. Amazingly, the official did nothing about it and when I went over to him he had a look of genuine fear in his eyes. There was the inevitable gamesmanship, when one of the Lazio players replaced the ball from the spot and put it just behind, in what I can only describe as a hole in the pitch. Colin Viljoen went to replace it again but the referee ordered him to take the kick and thankfully, despite the mayhem, he stayed calm to score.

The scenes that followed the goal were a disgrace to the game. With only about 17 minutes left on the clock it was clear that our away goal had made the Italians' task virtually impossible and they quickly wanted to take out their frustration. Trevor Whymark was targeted and chased by a player who attempted a scissor kick on him. Trevor ran all the way back and stood behind me, with his arms round my waist, and his attacker retreated. A Lazio supporter somehow managed to get on the pitch, despite the barbed wire and moat, but he was grabbed by several policemen before he could reach any of us.

Eight minutes before the end Chinaglia won himself a penalty when he got between Kevin Beattie and me, and kidded the referee that he had been fouled. He took it himself to make it 3-1 but we were still very much in the driving seat as far as the aggregate score was concerned. In the 87th minute he completed his hat-trick from another penalty and the home fans were going wild. But Lazio still needed another two goals to go through and with so little time left it looked as if we would just about hold on. By this time David Johnson was on for Woodsy – Jonty virtually begged the manager to let him have the last nine minutes or so – and in stoppage time he managed to score what was definitely the best goal of the game. He chested down Colin Viljoen's cross and his left-foot shot flew past their keeper. That made it 6-4 to us and it was a sweet moment for Jonty after what had happened to him in the first game.

The final whistle was a welcome sound but our problems were only just beginning. There were no handshakes between the players and the home fans were chucking all sorts of missiles on to the pitch. The Union Jack was also being burned and it was clear, yet again, that our supporters were being targeted. At least one of them needed hospital treatment and I'm surprised that David Best wasn't in the same boat as he literally took a kicking in the tunnel afterwards. Basically, their players went wild with rage and poor old

Besty was knocked to the floor, at which point about four or five of their lot proceeded to literally put the boot in. Fortunately, I spotted a pair of legs that I recognised as his and I waded in to drag him clear. Bobby Robson was nearby and shouted 'Don't you start anything, big man' which I thought was a bit rich in the circumstances.

I had to trade a few punches before I managed to get Besty into the dressing room and I was seething. I was all for getting a few of the lads together and going straight back out to get stuck into them, but the manager was having none of it and kept his back to the door to make sure none of us left. I'll never forget the look on his face. He was absolutely petrified. He'd been in football far longer than any of us and he had never seen anything like it. I can only describe the Lazio players as animals and what really got to me was that a number of armed policemen literally stood and watched the assault on Besty without doing anything to intervene. Also, where were the Lazio officials? I found myself trying to imagine the reverse situation at Portman Road and how it would have fizzled out in a matter of seconds. From what we could see, the club officials just seemed to accept it and allowed it to continue.

We locked ourselves in the dressing room as the banging on the door and the shouting continued. Cyril Lea, our coach, had a head count and the only person missing was the club doctor. By the time he turned up – more than an hour had elapsed before we heard a knock on the door followed by the sound of his voice – he was as white as a sheet. What we didn't know, while we were barricaded inside the dressing room, was that the riot police were using tear gas to disperse the home fans. Still the Lazio players kept kicking away at the door – they were baying for blood – until the noise eventually subsided. Almost two hours had elapsed before we made our move and we were ushered outside to the waiting bus. When I saw armed cops in Land Rover-type vehicles – one at the front, one at the back and one either side – I thought I was back in Belfast.

The coach was dark with its curtains drawn as we pulled away from the stadium and made our way back to the hotel. But as we got close we could see hundreds of Lazio supporters outside the hotel and the police pulled us over to say they were not prepared to risk taking us back there. So instead they took us up a mountain route to another hotel and it turned out to be full of Roma supporters, who welcomed us with open arms. The hotel staff managed to rustle up a meal for us and we spent virtually the whole night there before we got the all-clear to go back to our hotel. Some of us didn't even bother going to bed that night and even now it makes my blood boil that UEFA's punishment to Lazio amounted to a slap on the wrist, in the shape of a £1,500 fine and a year-long European ban. I'd have slung them out for good, the way I felt, and I think that went for everyone in the Ipswich party that night.

I had only been at the club for two years when it happened but I eventually stayed for 11, although in 1974 it looked as if I might have to move on. Bobby Robson has often said that I didn't know what I wanted and I fought tooth and nail to get it. It's a funny line but the truth of the matter is that I knew precisely what I wanted – to be treated with respect and to be given a fair deal. I'm sorry to say this, but I felt the manager was biased towards the English players in the team. In the summer of 1974 I decided I would have to move elsewhere unless I was paid what I felt I was worth. Let me make it quite clear that I was not being greedy because I knew perfectly well that the figure I was after was less than some of my colleagues were being paid.

When I first moved to Ipswich in 1971 I chose them ahead of both Leeds and Everton. I didn't want to go to Leeds because I had been over at Elland Road as a 17-year-old, when I was playing part-time for Coleraine and serving my apprenticeship as a carpenter. I didn't think the manager, Don Revie, had been fair with me and I had not forgotten it. I didn't fancy Everton either – I wanted to join Ipswich but I just wasn't 100 per cent sure where it was. I had a feeling it was near Colchester because a few years earlier I had played at Layer Road for Oldham. We stayed in a hotel at Bury St Edmunds and I was pretty sure I had seen signs for Ipswich as we made our way to Colchester on the day of the game. Carol hadn't a clue where it was so we got a map out so that we were absolutely sure of its exact location.

My first game for Town was a bit of a disaster as far as I was concerned. We lost 2-1 at home to Leicester and it definitely didn't go the way I'd have liked. I couldn't believe how quiet the Ipswich team were. It seemed I'd joined a team with no voices. Besty was in goal and I'd known him for years, since we were together at Oldham. I remember Leicester scoring past him and he was on the deck as I went into the net to retrieve the ball. I bent down and said to him 'I see you haven't improved' and it was said out of sheer frustration. I can't stress enough how disappointed I was with my debut. Under my breath I was muttering to myself 'What have I done, joining this shower of w*****s?' I really was that annoyed and in my mind it was clear why they were near the bottom of the league. I was relieved when things eventually picked up and I was ever-present through to the end of the season, then in the 1972-73 season I only missed one of the 54 games we played in all competitions as we finished fourth and qualified for Europe, little realising what lay in store for us.

Hard to believe, perhaps, but I signed for Ipswich for less money than I was earning at Blackburn, who had just been relegated to the Third Division. Playing in the First Division was what swung it for me, not the money. By the summer of 1974 I was pretty fed up. As far as I was concerned I wasn't being treated properly in terms of wages. I felt I had proved myself and at the risk of sounding big-headed, I genuinely believed the improvement in form, which resulted in us climbing the table, was at least partly down to me and the way I was playing for the team and the club. I was getting glowing references and I thought it was only right that I should be brought into line with the rest of the team.

In the end, when it seemed I was getting nowhere, I felt I had no alternative but to write a letter requesting a transfer. The first time I did it the manager asked me to see him in his office and he ripped the letter up in front of me. I went home and wrote another one and the very same thing happened all over again. My next move was to write to the chairman and this really got Bobby Robson's back up. He was absolutely raging at me for going to the chairman and I just told him 'What else could I do after you kept ripping up the letters I sent you?' He snapped and said 'Right, you're on the list' and the very next day he asked me to go to his office. When I walked in he said 'I've a man on the end of this phone who wants to talk to you'. It was Jimmy Bloomfield, the Leicester manager.

I spoke to him and he said he wanted to sign me for Leicester. Could I go up there and talk it through, he asked, and I ended up staying in the Holiday Inn for a couple of days with Carol and our only son at the time, Lee, who was very young. What puzzled me as I left Bobby Robson's office was that he said 'Go and see him by all means but don't you dare sign anything'. It seemed a strange thing to say because there was only one reason for me travelling to Leicester and that was to discuss a possible transfer. Jimmy Bloomfield and I sat down to discuss a deal and I was staggered when he offered me 75 per cent more than I was on at Ipswich. He was due to travel down to London with the team for a League Cup-tie at Arsenal and he suggested I accompany them to Highbury, while Carol and Lee stayed on at the hotel, but I didn't want to do that.

I got the impression that Jimmy Bloomfield was keen to complete a deal there and then, or at least to keep me away from Ipswich until I had signed. But we didn't want to hang around and instead we took ourselves over to

Coventry, where Ipswich were playing in a League Cup game. Bobby Robson had suggested I go over and by this time the news had become public knowledge. Several fans said 'Sorry to hear you're going' and 'We'll miss you' as I arrived in Coventry at the team's hotel and it was all a bit emotional. Bobby Robson and the players were having a pre-match meal and as soon as he clapped eyes on me he said 'What have you done?' I said I hadn't done anything and went on to tell him about Leicester's extremely generous offer, which was more than I was asking for at Ipswich. 'I don't see how they can do that,' he said and I assured him they were. 'You know what I want to stay and it's not as much as Leicester have offered me or what some of the other players are being paid,' I reminded him. Right there and then, he said 'Give me a minute' and he left me standing on my own while he was gone a lot longer than 60 seconds

I saw the manager talking to two directors, Murray Sangster and Harold Smith, over in the corner and they chatted for a few minutes before he returned to tell me 'You're on, you've got your contract'. I checked – 'It's what I asked for?' – and he confirmed it would be for that exact amount. He also shook my hand and said 'I'm glad you are staying'. I suppose the manager had backed himself into a corner and he knew that unless I got what I wanted I had a better offer up my sleeve from Leicester. When he confirmed the deal was on I was very pleased because deep down inside I didn't want to leave Ipswich. I'm sure a lot of players in my position would have signed the contract Leicester put in front of me but I can honestly say that throughout my career I never put money first. The one thing I couldn't understand was why the manager hadn't just agreed a new deal for me in the first place, some months earlier. I will always maintain, until my dying day, that I was not being treated fairly and I felt I had to make a stand.

Things couldn't have worked out much better than they did because Ipswich went from strength to strength in the next few years. The FA Cup win in 1978 was a massive highlight and after that I didn't play too many games. I accepted the player-manager's job at Colchester but within a few weeks I realised it wasn't for me. It seemed to be a 24-hours-a-day job and Carol noticed how much I changed in a short space of time. Once I decided to resign a lot of people told me the same – that I had become a different person as the pressure of management clearly got to me.

After working at Felixstowe Docks I received a call from Mike Walker after he had taken over as manager at Layer Road. I had got on well with Mike, who was a long-serving goalkeeper, in my time as manager and he asked me to go back as first team coach. I agreed and we were doing well when the club's new chairman decided to sack Mike. His timing was rather strange because a few days later Mike picked up the Manager of the Month award. I left at the same time and that was the end of me in football.

I have plenty of happy memories to look back on and only a few unpleasant ones, like that game in Lazio, which I remember for all the wrong reasons. Their big striker, Giorgio Chinaglia, went off to play in the North American Soccer League for New York Cosmos and one of my Northern Ireland colleagues, Dave Clements, who played for Coventry, Sheffield Wednesday and Everton, also went out there. Every time I saw Dave I used to tell him to take a message back over to 'Big George' telling him what I would do to him if I came across him again. It never happened and I doubt if it will now, so he's probably safe.

BRYAN HAMILTON
MIDFIELDER 1971–1975

BORN   31 December 1946, Belfast
SIGNED   12 August 1971 from Linfield, £30,000
IPSWICH CAREER   199 games, 56 goals
HONOURS   50 Northern Ireland caps
LEFT   Transferred to Everton, 27 November 1975; £40,000

Bryan was snapped up by Bobby Robson after starring for his country in the Home International Championship and the fee was a record for an Irish League player. He was the club's leading goalscorer in consecutive seasons, his knack of netting from midfield a useful weapon as Ipswich chased success at home and abroad. He helped Town to reach the FA Cup semi-finals in 1975 and he felt the defeat by West Ham in a Stamford Bridge replay more than most as he had a 'goal' controversially disallowed by referee Clive Thomas. Amazingly, the same official ruled out another FA Cup semi-final replay 'goal' two years later when Bryan netted for Everton against Liverpool and thought he had clinched the Toffees' place at Wembley. He twice returned to Portman Road in a coaching role and his club management career took in spells with Tranmere, Wigan, Leicester and Norwich, while he also took charge of his native Northern Ireland. He lives in Suffolk and is kept busy with a host of media commitments, as well as being technical advisor to the Antigua and Barbuda FA.

Ipswich Town 5 v Newcastle United 4

First Division
Saturday 15 March 1975

Portman Road
Attendance 23,070

Bryan scores his only hat-trick in senior football in a nine-goal thriller in the Portman Road mud as Ipswich continue their challenge for the First Division title

Teams

Bobby Robson	**Managers**	Joe Harvey
Laurie Sivell	1	Iam McFaul
George Burley	2	David Craig
Mick Mills	3	Micky Barker
Brian Talbot	4	Jimmy Smith
Allan Hunter	5	Aidan McCaffrey
Kevin Beattie	6	Irving Nattrass
		(Sub. Tommy Gibb)
Bryan Hamilton	7	Stewart Barraclough
Colin Viljoen	8	Geoff Nulty
David Johnson	9	Malcolm Macdonald
Trevor Whymark	10	John Tudor
Mick Lambert	11	Tommy Craig
Hamilton 4, 54, 64, Hunter 34, Johnson 51	Goals	Macdonald 7, 84, Tudor 21, 41

Referee: Keith Styles (Barnsley)

IT WAS AN EXCITING TIME for Ipswich Town in the mid-70s because under Bobby Robson's management the club was making year-on-year progress. From struggling to preserve First Division status during the early stages of his reign, we had reached the stage where we were seen as genuine challengers for the title. We were actually chasing a League Championship and FA Cup double in 1975, having finished fourth in the table in each of the previous two seasons. Interestingly, we were the only title candidates who reached the semi-finals of the FA Cup. We had emerged as a force to be reckoned with, spreading our wings into Europe, and the manager had assembled a squad that featured a number of international and soon-to-be capped players. I was delighted to be playing my part and I have chosen this particular match because I scored the only senior hat-trick of my career and it remains one of the most enthralling league fixtures to have taken place at Portman Road, a see-saw affair of which the outcome was in doubt right up until the final whistle.

Apart from their improving on-the-field fortunes, Ipswich were renowned at the time for having one of the finest pitches in the country, although on the day in question the weather had made it so heavy that in his programme article for the next home game, in which he reflected on what had occurred against Newcastle, the manager referred to the condition of the playing surface and admitted 'It was like a bog in the middle of the field.' He also talked about supporters being exhilarated by what they had witnessed, described my third goal, Town's fifth, as 'breathtaking' and admitted that he had been concerned by the team's defending in the first half, which ended with us trailing 3-2. 'A bit of stern talk at half-time,' said the manager 'righted the problem.' He also referred to the brace of goals by Malcolm Macdonald and added that they were 'as good a pair as one could ever wish to see.'

The week before we met Newcastle we drew 0-0 at home with a very powerful Leeds side in an FA Cup quarter-final tie. Portman Road was packed with a crowd of 38,010, a new record attendance that has never been bettered and could well stand for all time. In the replay at Elland Road, which took place the following Tuesday, we were leading thanks to a David

Johnson header until 20 seconds from the end of normal time when my future Everton team-mate, Duncan McKenzie, equalised. The game went into extra time and there was no further scoring. I mention that because it was hardly the ideal build-up to a league game we desperately wanted to win and which, given the strength-sapping conditions in which it was played, took the very maximum out of the players both mentally and physically. We had another two tilts with Leeds before we earned our semi-final place and with the title also a realistic proposition it would be no exaggeration to say we had a great deal on our plate at the time. In fact, it was so hectic that we played 10 games in the two major domestic competitions in the space of just 24 days – and we didn't have the squad numbers to allow the manager to rotate his players.

But we were delighted to be on a double mission, because for some clubs the season was virtually over. Note the crowd for the visit of Newcastle – almost 15,000 fewer fans than saw the Leeds tie, which I suppose shows how the FA Cup was very much the glamour competition back then. Those who did attend the Newcastle game certainly received value for money as it only cost 50p to stand on the terraces. An amazing game started with us claiming an early lead when Trevor Whymark headed down from a Mick Lambert left-wing cross. The ball literally got stuck in the mud six yards out and I was handily placed to shoot past Iam McFaul. Iam, or Willie as he was more popularly known, was a really nice lad and a decent keeper. He also happened to be related through marriage to our own Allan Hunter, whose brother Vic married the sister of Willie's wife, so there was a bit of good-natured 'feeling' that surrounded the game, what with us all being Northern Ireland international colleagues as well. Because of how events unfolded, there was plenty to talk about in the players' lounge afterwards.

Newcastle took only three minutes to equalise, Tommy Craig chipping the ball forward for Macdonald, who was in great form around that time, to blast a right-foot shot past Laurie Sivell. They were convinced they had gone ahead after 20 minutes when Geoff Nulty sent the ball high into the net from the edge of the box and they were none too pleased when the referee, after consulting his linesman, ruled no goal because not one, but two, Newcastle players were apparently offside. Nulty had better luck five minutes later as he headed across goal for John Tudor to nod home from close range. It was a significant goal as Newcastle became the first team that season to score twice in a First Division fixture at Portman Road but that was pretty soon forgotten as we made it 2-2. Poor Willie could only push a Mick Lambert cross into the air and who should be waiting to punish him but Allan Hunter, who headed the ball into the net. Four minutes before the interval Newcastle were back in front as Macdonald hit the ball low across goal for Tudor to net at the far post. It was pretty frantic and we needed the interval to get our breath back.

The amazing thing about our first-half display was that we conceded three goals in 45 minutes, because until then we had only leaked five in our previous 14 home games, which was a fantastic record. But within five minutes of the restart we were all-square again. George Burley and Allan Hunter were involved in the build-up and, no doubt helped by the state of the pitch, David Johnson's shot managed to creep under the keeper's body. Just three minutes later we were in front when I went to the near post and glided a header into the net from Mick Lambert's cross on the left. It was a favourite trick of mine to get in there and try to nick a goal. Macdonald almost made it 4-4 when he headed against the bar and within seconds we went to the other end and made it 5-3. I raced away, went round 17-year-old Aiden McCaffrey, who was making his senior debut, and shot low into the far corner. Six minutes from the end Macdonald completed the scoring with a terrific shot high into the net but to be honest we played out the remaining time not knowing what the final result might be. They had chances to not only peg us back, but possibly even go on to win the game, while we were also close to scoring a sixth goal.

THERE WAS A FEELING of both delight and relief in the home dressing room at the end. It had been a real see-saw affair and I remember Newcastle manager Joe Harvey summing up his frustration when he said 'This club is jinxed. We are not meant to win anything.' Fast forward 35 years and the Geordies still haven't put that right, for one reason or another. But on that day they were difficult opponents and Macdonald must have been hard pushed to accept he was a loser because he scored two crackers and was very much the country's most in-form striker at the time. Newcastle also believed that having to put ex-Burnley midfielder Nulty into defence to replace the injured Irving Nattrass, who failed to appear in the second half, proved costly. Their reasoning was that the switch allowed our own Colin Viljoen, who went on to win England honours that season, to take charge of that area having been kept pretty quiet by Nulty in an extremely eventful first period.

Newcastle coach Keith Burkinshaw, who later managed Tottenham, claimed afterwards that my third goal was a fluke. According to him, my shot was going wide but hit a divot to divert the ball just inside the far post. I couldn't really say one way or the other, but there is no doubt that the muddy pitch added to the entertainment value because it made life difficult for defenders and other players were not at their best either. I have to say it suited me because I was athletic, busy, could get about and had strong legs. It was my type of game. It ebbed and flowed, and the important thing from our point of view was the result, as it kept us in the hunt for the title. From a purely personal point of view, I was elated to have scored my first hat-trick. I was our leading scorer that season, as well as in the previous campaign, and as a midfield player I took a lot of pleasure from that. Midfield goals are a bonus to any side. I remember clutching the match ball at the end and I couldn't really believe it when I heard Bobby Robson saying 'What's he doing with the ball?' Even now, I'm not sure if he was joking, hadn't realised I had scored three, or whether he was trying to save the club a few quid. First team coach Cyril Lea stepped in and said 'Boss, he got a hat-trick' and I made off with the ball, which I still have among my many souvenirs, before anyone could stop me.

The following Tuesday we went to Stoke and won, which put us second in the league, but although we only suffered one defeat in our last 10 games it still wasn't enough. Derby were crowned champions with Liverpool and Ipswich both two points worse off. Had it been goal difference that separated sides back then we would have been runners-up by a margin of one goal, but because it was goal average we had to settle for third place. What happened to us in the FA Cup was also disappointing, or should I say devastating, because we eventually got past Leeds in a third replay but went out in a semi-final replay to West Ham that was one of the worst experiences of my entire career. I even shudder now as I recall it. But first of all let's go back to our fifth round tie at home to Aston Villa, who were then in the Second Division.

This was a game that I considered selecting, but since I only appeared as a second-half substitute it didn't seem right. Around that time I was actually out of the starting line-up. I had been injured and then, once I was fully fit again, I could not dislodge the man who had replaced me, Roger Osborne. We went into the Villa game with two out-and-out wingers in Clive Woods and Mick Lambert, which was rare for us, and it looked as if we might be going out of the competition as we were trailing 1-0 at half-time and then conceded another goal four minutes after the restart. At that point I remember Cyril gesturing up to the manager, who was sitting in the directors' box, in a bid to get me on. David Johnson actually pulled one back before the manager decided things were sufficiently desperate for me to replace Woodsy with about 15 minutes left on the clock.

I scored twice to put us into the quarter-finals and found myself in demand for the after-match interviews, which were much more low-key than they are today. I admit I was an arrogant little so-and-so and I told the reporters that I just wanted to play and if it wasn't going to be at Ipswich then it would have to be somewhere else. Monday's papers all carried head-lines along the lines of 'Hamilton still not happy' and the manager wasted no time in getting me into his office. Honestly, he gave me such a tongue-lashing. But my two-goal display against Villa at least saw me recalled to the side and I started every game through to the end of the season. I don't want to sound big-headed, but I could always nick a goal and in a way it was my trademark. In the three seasons between 1972 and 1975 I scored 50 goals in 158 appearances, which was a pretty good ratio for a midfield player.

In the Northern Ireland team I played more of an attacking role on the right with Derek Dougan our leading striker and George Best supposedly on the left, although a player as good as Besty was basically left to do what he wanted. I liked to hover in the right areas and I wasn't afraid to gamble. Ipswich played Sheffield United on one occasion and they had a player called Geoff Salmon, who was told to pick me up and stuck to me like glue. I managed to get to the near post and knock one in, and he only missed me by inches. As I picked myself up I remember him saying 'You little bastard – you're going to get me slaughtered at half-time.' I recognised I was no six-foot plus striker and while I could head the ball I wasn't in the same league as others, like Kevin Beattie, Allan Hunter, David Johnson or Trevor Whymark, who was one of the very best I ever saw in the air. I was an opportunist and I thought it made sense to stick to what I was good at.

THERE ARE A COUPLE OF good stories that tend to sum up me, and my goalscoring, pretty well. I was playing for Northern Ireland against Yugoslavia in April 1975, the first game back in Belfast after a four-year gap, and the atmosphere was highly charged. I'll never forget big Hunter, who was never afraid to go in where it hurt, challenging for a header at the far post and the ball dropping for me to prod it over the line for the only goal of the game. In my mind it was a skill to be in the right place at the right time. A similar thing happened when Ipswich played Birmingham City, whose keeper was Dave Latchford. We had a corner from which Kevin Beattie got in a looping header and as the ball started to come down all the other players were moving out. 'No,' I thought to myself and I instead moved closer towards the goal. Dave tipped the ball against the bar and as it dropped I nodded it over the line from about six inches. As I always said, I was absolutely lethal from that range.

Having joined the club in 1971 I was fortunate enough to see the team evolve. Allan Hunter arrived to give us a presence we had been lacking and young players like Kevin Beattie and George Burley began to emerge. We had tricky wingers in Woods and Lambert, a striker in David Johnson who was as quick with the ball at his feet as he was without it and another in Trevor Whymark, who was virtually without equal when it came to aerial ability. In midfield we had the wonderful range of passing, short and long, offered by Colin Viljoen and Peter Morris. It was good to see it coming together and to be a part of it. Believe me, nobody liked playing Ipswich and I remember top managers like Bill Nicholson and Bill Shankly admitting it. I suppose I took it as an affront if I wasn't in the side. I wanted to play every single game, often to my detriment, and it was only when I became a manager that I fully appreciated how difficult it was to keep everyone happy and the many other problems that went with the job.

I had a wonderful career but it still hurts that I was denied an FA Cup Final appearance. I believe I should have done it with Ipswich and again with Everton. Two refereeing decisions – made by the very same official, Clive Thomas – hit me very hard. In 1975 our workload was such that we had a lot of injuries to contend with as we faced West Ham in the semi-final at Villa Park. We drew 0-0 and we still had problems for the replay just four days later at Stamford Bridge, where both Hunter and Johnson were missing. But we were still the better team and no-one will ever convince me that but for the referee chalking off my early 'goal' we would not have gone on to win the trophy against Fulham at Wembley. When the ball hit the net I did what I always did, glanced over to the linesman to make sure all was well before I started celebrating. On this occasion the linesman was on his way back to the half-way line – it was clearly a perfectly good goal. But the referee had other ideas and later explained there had been an infringement, which could mean anything and at the time it seemed to me to be the perfect get-out clause.

Thomas used the word infringement again two years later when I was playing for Everton against Liverpool in a semi-final staged at Maine Road, Manchester. I had gone on for Martin Dobson and six minutes from the end Ronnie Goodlass sent over a cross that Duncan McKenzie flicked on with his head. I was poaching right in front of goal and the ball came to me at an awkward height but I managed to nudge it over the line with my hip.

Liverpool defenders Emlyn Hughes and Joey Jones were nearby and did nothing to protest, while I looked over to see the linesman and he was on his way towards the half-way line. It was a goal and we were going to Wembley, I thought to myself. But Thomas, who I estimate was 25 yards away, blew his whistle and ruled no goal. He thought he knew better and to this day my hunch is that he was thinking to himself 'How did he turn the ball in if he didn't use his arm?' He thought he was ahead of the game and second-guessed the situation – but he got it wrong. To my knowledge the only person at both Stamford Bridge and Maine Road who saw anything wrong with my 'goals' was Thomas. We were suddenly denied the win we deserved and we lost the replay 3-0.

I MAY HAVE ONLY become a full-time footballer when I joined Ipswich at the age of 24 but my career had been pretty eventful up until then. I had my international experience and in 1967 had also reached the quarter-finals of the European Cup with Linfield. I scored in a 2-2 draw with CSKA Sofia at Windsor Park and we lost by the only goal in the return leg in Bulgaria. Had we reached the semi-final we would have played Inter Milan, who famously went on to be beaten by Celtic in the final. My father had encouraged me to complete my education – I worked with computers as an electrical engineer – before turning to football. Back in Belfast I was obsessed with the idea of making it in England and I was determined to push myself as far as I could. Other players back home were quite happy to combine playing with another job, but not me and I couldn't have done much more to push myself. Incidentally, this will interest Ipswich fans who remember Allan Hunter for the great defender he undoubtedly was – when I first played against him he was a useful midfield player with very good feet for a tall guy.

In 1971, when I moved to England, I had several other clubs interested in signing me but everything about Ipswich seemed right and I never regretted my decision. Four years later I was off and I have to confess I was surprised. I felt I was being squeezed out. Roger Osborne, a smashing lad and unbelievably nice man, was seen as an adequate replacement and I moved to Everton where Billy Bingham, who had been my manager with Linfield and Northern Ireland, was in charge. I fancied a crack at playing with a big city club and after that I moved to Millwall, where I suffered yet more FA Cup frustration. I was captain the day Ipswich beat us 6-1 at The Den in 1978. Town were a fantastic side and far too good for us on the day, but it was the crowd trouble that stopped play that really affected me. I thought it was totally unacceptable and I made up my mind to move on to the next phase of my career. I joined Swindon as player-coach then I moved back to Merseyside as player-manager of Tranmere, before moving to take charge of Wigan and Leicester.

I succeeded Billy Bingham as Northern Ireland manager and I suppose you could say I was on a mission. I was aware of Billy's plans to retire and when the opportunity came along I jumped at it. I saw myself as an ambassador for the country and although we had some good results during my time in charge, the lack of a goalscorer meant we were never able to take the extra step and qualify for the final stages of either the European Championship or the World Cup. I lost my job but I have no bitterness within me. There were a great deal of positives that came out of my time as national manager and I will always be grateful for having had the opportunity. I love a challenge and late in 1997 Ipswich manager George Burley asked me to join him as first team coach. Town were fourth from bottom at the time but we tweaked the team a little bit. I felt we lacked a bit of pace in the middle of the park and pushed for Kieron Dyer to be a regular choice. George pulled off a real coup with the signing of David Johnson from Bury and a run of just one defeat in 23 games during the second half of the league programme saw us qualify for the play-offs, where we lost to Charlton. I was working without a contract and although people recognised that I had influenced what had taken place, no one said anything about a contract and whether or not I would be continuing my role into the following season. On the back of what I had done with both Northern Ireland and Ipswich I had about five or six job offers, including one from Norwich that I accepted.

I went to Carrow Road on a three-year contract as director of football, a role that combined working with the first team and helping to build the academy set-up. I took over as manager when things weren't as they should have been at first team level and my first game in charge, in March 2000, was against Ipswich at Portman Road, which we won 2-0. However, I never felt it was going to be long-term at Norwich because some people could not change their perception of me as an Ipswich Town person. I was thoroughly professional and gave it 100 per cent but some people were unwilling to forgive or forget and I resigned in December 2000. I returned to Ipswich, again as first team coach, in the 2001-2002 season and although we managed to put together a run of seven wins from eight Premiership games, to suggest we could avoid relegation, we suffered a damaging 6-0 home defeat to Liverpool from which we never really recovered. That game was followed by a three-week break brought about by international fixtures and when we regrouped we could not recapture our earlier impressive form. We managed just one win in the last 12 league games and were duly relegated, and as someone without a contract I was an easy target. To this day I am desperately disappointed that it didn't work out.

I now have a number of media commitments, including a role as a summariser for BBC Radio Five. I also do some television work, but I much prefer radio, because I believe it is about painting pictures for people and trying to make that picture as clear as possible. Radio has been my friend in the car for many years and I like to think I talk the language of the people. The job as technical advisor to the Antigua and Barbuda FA keeps me involved on the inside of the game too. I am helping them to put in place an academy structure and it is going well. I also make motivational speeches and when I look back on my time in football – I was a player until the age of 38, then I spent over 20 years in coaching and management – I realise how fortunate I have been. I don't hold grudges – not even against Clive Thomas!

ROGER OSBORNE
MIDFIELDER 1971–1981

BORN 9 March 1950, Otley, Suffolk
SIGNED 12 October 1971, from amateur
IPSWICH CAREER 149 games, 10 goals
HONOURS FA Cup 1978
LEFT Transferred to Colchester, February 1981, £25,000

Roger's dream of becoming a professional footballer had long since passed when, at the age of 21, he chauffeured his younger brother David to evening training sessions at Portman Road. Invited to make up the numbers for the Ipswich second string, he was then given a full-time contract and went on to become an established member of Bobby Robson's senior squad. The fairytale was not complete, however, until he scored the winning goal in the 1978 FA Cup Final to clinch victory over red-hot favourites Arsenal. Until being signed by Town he maintained a family tradition by turning out for Westerfield United, members of the Suffolk and Ipswich League, and it was with the same club that he played his final games, by which time his son Robert was also in the side. Roger also played for Colchester and then represented Sudbury, Braintree and Felixstowe, demonstrating a true love of the game. After football he had a number of jobs before becoming manager of the Rushmere Sports Centre in Ipswich, a post he has held for 10 years.

Ipswich Town 1 v Arsenal 0

FA Cup Final
Saturday 6th May 1978

Wembley Stadium
Attendance 100,000

*Ipswich mark their first Wembley appearance by winning the FA Cup
and take the famous old trophy back to Suffolk for the first time
to amazing scenes*

Teams

Bobby Robson	**Managers**	Terry Neill
Paul Cooper	1	Pat Jennings
George Burley	2	Pat Rice
Mick Mills	3	Sammy Nelson
Brian Talbot	4	David Price
Allan Hunter	5	David O'Leary
Kevin Beattie	6	Willie Young
Roger Osborne	7	Liam Brady
(Sub. Mick Lambert)		(Sub. Graham Rix)
John Wark	8	Alan Sunderland
Paul Mariner	9	Malcolm Macdonald
David Geddis	10	Frank Stapleton
Clive Woods	11	Alan Hudson
Osborne 77	Goal	

Referee: Derek Nippard (Bournemouth)

I SHOULD PROBABLY START by saying a very sincere thank-you to those players who were my team-mates at the FA Cup Final in 1978, some of whom are featured elsewhere in this book – not only for helping to make my dream come true back then but also for agreeing to select other games so that I could have this one as the Match of My Life. It most certainly was, for reasons that must be glaringly obvious, since it outshone all others as the biggest highlight of my career. Even now, 30 years later, there are times when I still can hardly believe what happened to me in the space of seven amazing, some might say crazy, days.

In order to make you appreciate what being part of a winning Wembley side is like, never mind the unbelievable high of scoring the only goal, I need to kick-off my recollection at Villa Park one week earlier. Ipswich were away to Aston Villa in a league fixture, our very last game before facing Arsenal in the FA Cup Final, and for that reason alone it was a key game. Paul Cooper and Paul Mariner sat it out as they nursed minor injuries, but both players knew their Wembley places were secure. My situation was far less clear-cut as manager Bobby Robson dropped me to the bench and recalled Colin Viljoen in my place, which plunged me into a period of great uncertainty.

Every time I recall what happened at Villa Park I say the same thing – I was in a state of shock. There is no better way that I can describe my feelings. I was numb with shock, utterly speechless, although a thousand and one things were racing through my mind at the same time. What did this mean? Were my chances of playing in the final virtually nil now that Viljoen was back after injury? Would I even be substitute at Wembley? Maybe the manager would prefer a more attacking player on the bench, leaving me with a seat in the stand. At that time I could not get it out of my head that my one and only chance of playing in the showpiece, end-of-season game had been blown to smithereens.

It was sheer agony to sit there in the dressing room beforehand and agonise about my possible fate. I tried not to, but it was impossible and I guarantee it would be the same for anyone else put in that terrible position. No matter how hard I tried to concentrate on that day's game, my mind

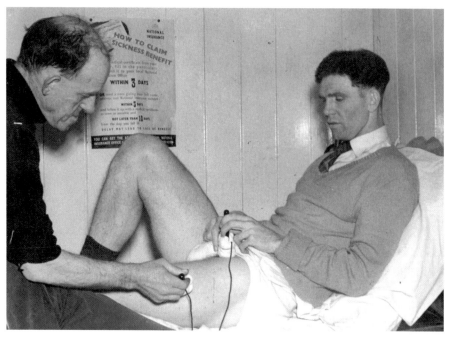

Check out the sign on the wall as I receive treatment
from Ipswich trainer Jimmy Forsyth.

It's 1953 and I am pictured (second from right) with Ipswich forward line
colleagues Billy Reed, Alec Crowe, Tom Garneys and George McLuckie.

The Ipswich Town squad that clinched the club's first major honour, the Third Division (South) Championship, in 1954.
Back row, left to right, Billy Reed, Jim Feeney, Tom Garneys, Jack Parry, George McLuckie, John Elsworthy and Doug Rees.
Front row, Scott Duncan (Manager), Basil Acres, Alec Crowe, Tommy Parker, Neil Myles, Tom Brown and Jimmy Forsyth (Trainer).

It's 2008 now and I am showing off my unique collection of medals for winning the Third Division (South) twice, the Second Division and the First Division.

That's yours truly, second from left on the back row, of what was our recognised first team line-up in the League Championship-winning season, 1961/62. The other players are, back row, left to right, John Compton, Bill Baxter, Andy Nelson, Ray Crawford, Jimmy Leadbetter and John Elsworthy. Front row, Doug Moran, Ted Phillips, Roy Bailey and Roy Stephenson.

That's me in action at Fulham's Craven Cottage in October 1962.

The man who signed me and made it all possible – Alf Ramsey.

The warm-up gives me a chance to practice my shooting.

That's skipper Andy Nelson on the left and my scoring partner, Ray Crawford, on the right as we toast our League Championship success.

After winning the League title in 1962, Ipswich met Floriana in the European Cup. Here I challenge goalkeeper Lolly Debastitta to score one of our goals in the 4-1 first leg victory in Malta.

Ted Phillips and I pictured in our heyday at Ipswich.

The Ipswich first team at the start of the 1961/62 season. Ken Malcolm (second from right in back row) was unfortunate to be injured three games in and John Compton replaced him.

My team-mates John Compton, Roy Bailey, Andy Nelson,
Roy Stephenson and Ted Phillips show off the League Championship
trophy to supporters on a crowded Cornhill.

It's 2007 and my former team-mate and good friend, Ted Phillips, and I
have just become inaugural members of the Ipswich Town Hall of Fame.

That's me on the extreme left, claiming offside as we try to keep out Manchester United pair Denis Law and Brian Kidd during my Old Trafford debut.

Ipswich skipper Mick Mills is under pressure from Brian Kidd during our victory at United.

This is how I looked back in 1974, by which time I was established in the Ipswich first team.

With David Geddis (left), celebrating victory at Wembley in 1978.

This action shot was taken in the mid-1970s.

I am followed out of the tunnel by David Johnson (left) and Paul Cooper.
Captaining Ipswich was a pleasure and a privilege.

Lifting the FA Cup (above) and the UEFA Cup (below) were the greatest moments of my Ipswich career.

My long hair is not the only major clue that this picture was taken in the mid-70s. That typically muddy pitch is another real giveaway.

Our first glimpse of the intimidating Olympic Stadium in Rome ahead of the controversial UEFA Cup clash with Lazio in 1973 was for this training session the afternoon before the game.

European action in 1977 as I take on Barcelona and Holland star Johan Cruyff, the number one player in the world at that time.

A change of kit to all-blue in this away game.

This tackle on me by Kevin Keegan would probably
mean an instant red card these days.

Another goal, this time in our 4-1 win at Luton in September 1974.

I'm in the number seven shirt as Kevin Beattie climbs to power in a header during that unforgettable 5-4 win over Newcastle.

It's 2001 and I am back at Portman Road as first team coach.

Paul Mariner is tackled by Arsenal defender David O'Leary
during the 1978 FA Cup Final.

Pat Jennings collects the ball on this occasion,
but I eventually got the better of him.

Celebrating my goal and it is clear I am already close to collapsing. I was in such a state – a mixture of elation and exhaustion – that I had to be substituted (below) and our coach, Cyril Lea, helped me off the pitch.

The FA Cup is finally ours as we pose for pictures.

Kevin Beattie, Paul Cooper and David Geddis celebrate with Robin Turner, who did a terrific job in the earlier rounds.

Wembley and the FA Cup Final becomes reality after my last-gasp header sees off West Bromwich Albion in the semi-final at Highbury.

Here I am trying a left-foot shot in the away leg of the UEFA Cup Final against AZ Alkmaar in 1981.

I'm about to join the celebrations after Frans Thijssen puts us ahead just three minutes into the second leg of the UEFA Cup Final in 1981.

It didn't feel like we were in Amsterdam with around 10,000 Ipswich fans there to cheer us on.

We were already 4-1 ahead going into the home leg of the UEFA Cup quarter-final against St Etienne in 1981.

Hard to believe now maybe, but Ipswich thumped Manchester United 6-0 at Portman Road in March 1980 and that's me celebrating one of my two goals.

It's 1982 and no doubt my five goals against Southampton helped to land me the supporters' Player of the Year award (right), which I received from director and former chairman John Cobbold.

A typical action shot as I am confronted by a defender – and don't you think the ball we used in those days was a bit ahead of its time?

This picture is from the 1992/93 season when Ipswich were members of the inaugural Premier League.

One of the biggest games of my Ipswich career – the 1-1 draw at Oxford in April 1992 that guaranteed we would become Second Division champions.

I was only 16 when I scored my first Ipswich goal, but a fair bit older in this shot as I challenge Sean Flynn as the two teams clash in the Masters.

I've just converted from the spot against Bolton to cancel out their early opener and (below) Matt Holland is quick to congratulate me.

Jamie Clapham salutes the crowd after converting the penalty
I wanted to take.

Jubilant fans enjoy our victory over Bolton and are already
looking ahead to the play-off final at Wembley.

I'm up above the Barnsley defenders to meet Jim Magilton's cross
and head us level at Wembley.

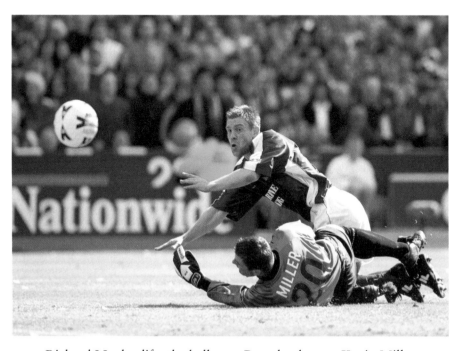

Richard Naylor lifts the ball over Barnsley keeper Kevin Miller
to put us ahead soon after half-time

Marcus Stewart puts us 3-1 ahead in the play-off final at Wembley – but we still had to hang on anxiously before the final whistle.

It's all over and the sheer relief is obvious as I join the other Wembley goalscorers, Richard Naylor, Martijn Reuser and Marcus Stewart.

Text-book stuff – head down, eye on the ball – as I
crack in a half-volley.

It's time to celebrate after scoring the first of my three goals
against Bristol City.

The hat-trick is complete and (below) I milk the applause
of the Portman Road crowd.

could not stop me from looking ahead seven days and every time I thought about it, even as the game against Villa got under way, I convinced myself that I would be one of the 100,000 spectators at the final, rather than in the thick of the action out on the pitch.

Basically, the manager wanted to give Viljoen a chance to show what he could do. He had been sidelined with injury for a couple of months and was keen to grab his chance, which was understandable, and he was probably thinking it was make or break depending on what happened in the game against Villa. As for me, I genuinely feared the worst. I couldn't get it out of my head that if Viljoen played well he would also be in the team for Wembley. It wouldn't matter that I had played more than twice as many games as he had, including 14 on the trot until that time. It was unquestionably the worst I ever felt throughout my time in football and I was told later by some of the other players that when Bobby Robson said "I'm leaving you out today, Roger" the colour drained from my face and I looked as if I had seen a ghost.

The other players, with the obvious exception of Viljoen, were also in a state of shock as they tried to come to terms with the manager's reshuffle of the side. I was the one to suffer most, by being left out completely, but my midfield colleague, John Wark, was surprised to be asked to play on the right of midfield, a role he had never occupied before. The decision clearly angered a number of the players. They maybe didn't say a great deal but the look on their faces said it all. It was the weirdest dressing-room atmosphere I ever experienced and in the middle of it all was 17 year-old goalkeeper Paul Overton, preparing for his senior debut and probably wondering what he had got caught up in. It clearly affected the group in a very negative way as they plummeted o a 6-1 defeat to Villa, hardly the ideal preparation for the following week's visit to Wembley.

Looking back, I can appreciate what the manager was doing. Viljoen was a quality player and one who had served the club well for the bulk of his 10 years at Portman Road. He had played his way into the England set-up three years earlier, when he was clearly one of the most influential midfielders around. Maybe the manager felt Viljoen, as a fine passer of the ball, was the right man to exploit the bigger-than-average playing area at Wembley. But that argument was flawed, at least in my mind and that of several, if not all, of the other Ipswich players. They knew that Viljoen would not want to man-mark Liam Brady and Town might have a lot to lose by allowing the Irishman to run riot if he was afforded such freedom.

Rightly or wrongly, I had taken it for granted that I would be playing against Arsenal – until the manager axed me from the line-up at Villa Park, that is. I had been a regular in the side and I could think of no reason why I would not continue along similar lines at Wembley. I am one of 12 children and you might recall the BBC commentator, David Coleman, making a big thing of that as we went up to receive the trophy from HRH Princess Alexandra. He said the family had hired a bus to transport everyone to London and he was spot-on. But what he didn't know was that I also had relatives coming from all over the country – Birmingham, Cornwall etc – to see me play in the biggest game of my career. I was banking on getting more than 60 tickets to keep everyone happy and shortly after receiving the dreaded news that I was being dropped I was asking myself if I would have to contact a lot of them and tell them two things – I wasn't going to be playing and I couldn't supply the tickets either.

The more I think about the events of 1978, the more I believe the manager fell into the same trap as many of his counterparts have done over the years. Steve McClaren, when he was in charge of England, for example. He wanted to play his best players, when he should have played his best team. There's a big difference and McClaren paid with his job. What if Ipswich had won at Villa Park that day? Would Bobby Robson have changed the team again? I very much doubt it. I'm convinced it would have made up his mind for him that he had done the right thing restoring Viljoen and he'd have stuck with him at Wembley. Paul Cooper and Paul Mariner, who both missed the Villa game because of minor injuries, would have been recalled but I'd have been left out. Would Ipswich still have won the FA Cup? That's something we'll never know but clearly I wouldn't have been able to score the winner.

In a sense, the whole situation turned upside down as a result of the result against Villa. The experiment – I think that's the right word – failed and it was almost a case of back to the drawing board. Well, not exactly, because the manager made the position quite clear when we were back in the dressing room afterwards. He hadn't said a word to me the whole 90 minutes but once the game was over he said 'Roger is the only one to come out of this with any credit'. It wasn't his intention, I don't think, but that told me all I needed to know and from that moment on I knew I would be in the team seven days later to face Arsenal. The manager didn't have to say anything else, either indirectly or to my face. The argument as to whether it would be me or Viljoen playing at Wembley had come and gone, and there could only be one outcome as far as I could see. There was absolutely no way he could risk taking the very same chance in the final, was there? I convinced myself he couldn't and the rest of the players saw it that way, too.

OVER THE NEXT FEW DAYS, as the build-up to the big game got under way in earnest, it was clear that the manager's mind was made up. He still didn't come to me and confirm anything – for example he never pulled me to one side and said 'You're definitely playing' – but I just knew. I had gone from being in a position where I doubted if I would even make the bench to knowing I would start the game and I have to confess it was a wonderful feeling. The more we worked on the tactics we were going to deploy against Arsenal – who would be marking who, that sort of thing – the more I realised I was to be involved from the start and the sheer relief I felt is really hard to put into words.

It's the same when you take an overview of my career. I think everybody knows by now how I came to be signed by Ipswich. I was giving my younger brother, David, a lift to training sessions at Portman Road in the hope that he would be taken on. I was 21 and working on a building site at the time. I played for Westerfield United in the Suffolk and Ipswich League, and to be perfectly honest my day-dreaming days had long since passed. As kids, all we did in our spare time was kick a ball around and pretend to be either Ray Crawford or Ted Phillips. We all wanted to be footballers back then but as a working man I never gave it a second thought that my dream could still come true. Let's be honest, you wouldn't, would you?

I used to sit and watch as David joined other hopefuls who had been invited to train one night a week. One week I was asked if I fancied joining in, so that's what I did. It turned out they had a lot of injuries and were struggling for bodies to put in the reserves. Geoff Hammond knew me and put a word in, so I've got a lot to be grateful to him for. I was earning £25 a week on the building site and when Town said I would get £15 to play in the reserves I was well pleased. I remember playing against the big clubs, like Arsenal, Chelsea and Tottenham, in what was then the Football Combination, and it was a very high standard compared to what I was used to locally. One thing simply led to another and I was offered a full-time professional contract at £25, so when I signed it I actually became worse off. But you don't turn down a chance like that, do you?

At that point I hadn't a clue what the future held in store and I certainly didn't allow myself to even consider the possibility of playing, never mind scoring the winning goal, in the FA Cup Final. To be honest, Ipswich weren't a club in those days that you would consider as possible FA Cup winners. They were outsiders – but all that was about to change. If I remember correctly, I was paid a bonus of £2 for a win and £1 for a draw when I was playing for the reserves. I think the best salary I had at Portman Road was about 12 grand a year and I did my sums one day when I was reading about today's Premiership salaries to work out that top stars like Steven Gerrard, Wayne Rooney and Frank Lampard earn more in a week than I did in my entire career. But my story is not about money. I've seen it described as a fairytale in some newspapers and I suppose it's difficult to argue with that description. Also, Bobby Robson once said that if they took my story to Hollywood they would say it was a little far-fetched, and I wouldn't dispute it.

THE GREAT THING ABOUT our FA Cup win in 1978 is that it was the first time Ipswich had done it and, for all we know, it might turn out to be the only time it ever happens. I sincerely hope not, but you never know. From my point of view, the fact that I scored the only goal was the icing on the cake. Any goal would have been a bonus and even if I hadn't scored I'd have been thrilled to come away with a winner's medal. But every now and again, when something jogs my memory, like a mention of the FA Cup on television or an article in the paper, I still find it hard to believe that I actually scored the only goal. Clearly, that is something only a few players can say they did. I can't deny it meant an awful lot to me to do it, and still does, because I had absolutely no reputation as a goalscorer – the Wembley winner was only my second goal in 37 first team appearances that season.

Actually, that is not strictly true. The record books say I netted twice that season but I actually scored three times. The one that got away was the late equaliser at Bristol Rovers when we seemed to be heading out of the FA Cup. All I did was help the ball over the line – it was going in anyway – from Robin Turner's shot. Robin also scored our first goal at Eastville and I was quite happy for him to get the credit for both. Funnily enough, the Bristol keeper said afterwards that I had scored it and he was right, but nobody paid any attention and I said nothing. I've stayed quiet until now and in setting the record straight I'm not looking to take anything away from Robin or ask for the records to be amended. These days, players claim goals for the slightest of touches, but strictly speaking it was my goal at Bristol as I definitely got the very last touch before it went over the line.

As for me scoring the only goal in a game, I have checked the record books – it didn't take too long – and I managed to score the only goal in a game on just one other occasion during my time at Portman Road. That was against Birmingham City at St Andrew's in December 1974, just a couple of days after we lost to Luton on Boxing Day, a result that was to cost us the League Championship that season. The point I'm making is that I was not a regular marksman, the way Paul Mariner and John Wark were, so to actually be the scorer of the Wembley winner was something it took a while to come to terms with. At least it helps people to remember I was in the team because they tend not to forget the goalscorer, but I have always said that if we had lost to Arsenal people would be able to name the other 10 members of the Ipswich team before me. It would be my name they would struggle with because I was a sort of background figure, an unsung hero if you like, and it never really bothered me that I wasn't in the limelight.

Scoring the goal didn't change me. I'm still the same bloke I've always been and that's something I am proud of. My job for the past ten years has been to manage a local sports centre but we don't have a big staff and I do a bit of everything. We had some kids in there one day and word must have got round that I used to play the game. I overheard a lad say to his mate 'If he's a former footballer, how come he is sweeping out the dressing room?' The answer is that I have to work for a living, but good luck to today's stars if they have enough money tucked away for when they retire. It wasn't like that in the 70s, whether you scored the winning goal in the FA Cup Final or not.

My role on the day was to man-mark Liam Brady. It was a job that I had grown accustomed to – I even had the honour of marking Johan Cruyff when he was at Barcelona and probably the best player in the world at the time – but it wasn't something I did in every game I played. The manager's decision to bring in David Geddis to play wide on the right had a big part to play in our success that day. In a sense David was doing my old job for the team, but doing it further up the pitch in order to curb the threat presented by Sammy Nelson, the Gunners' left-back who tended to launch a lot of their attacks. That allowed me to tuck in and mark Brady, which made my job easier. When I played wide on the right I would switch between marking their midfield player and their full-back, and our right-back, George Burley, would do the same, but in the plan drawn up by the manager and his staff I could concentrate on one job. People were quick to say that Brady wasn't 100 per cent fit and I would have to agree. In fact, he maybe regretted playing in the first place, but don't forget that we were unaware of his fitness until the game started.

Our biggest problem on the day was turning our possession into goals. Everything about our game was spot-on but when it came to putting the ball in the net our luck seemed to be out. Paul Mariner hit the bar, John Wark struck the same post twice and George Burley was denied by a truly world class save by a world class goalkeeper in Pat Jennings. It felt as if it was only a matter of time before we did score, but on the other hand when the clock is ticking away and there are only about 13 minutes of the 90 left you wouldn't be human if you didn't at least wonder if it simply wasn't going to be your day. We were so much on top it was quite incredible. Arsenal were not able to offer very much in the way of real threat. It certainly wasn't an end-to-end game – it was literally one-sided – but the longer you go without scoring the more you start to think they might just have one attack, score and see the game out. Fortunately, that didn't happen.

The move that led to our goal was started by Clive Woods. For some reason, our left-winger was wide on the right, and he tried to hit a pass in to me that rebounded off Alan Hudson. Woodsy had a second chance and this time he gave it to David Geddis, who was in a perfect position to take on Nelson. By this time we had bodies further up the pitch and when David beat Nelson he hit the ball low and hard across the face of the goal. Maybe it could have been a better cross – he might have cut it back – but when Willie Young got a foot to the ball it actually did us a favour. He was only able to knock it out to me and I had to react quickly. Just as well, perhaps, because if I'd had time to think the moment would have gone. In the second or so that I had to think my only thought was to keep my shot low. You often see players shoot well over the bar from that sort of opportunity and I was determined that wasn't going to happen to me.

I had no choice but to hit it with my 'other' foot, my left. I'm pretty sure I never scored another goal with my left foot, so that's another bonus in a way. Bobby Robson was always on at me to use my left foot more, so a lot of the credit should go to him. I did manage to keep the ball low and it struck me afterwards, when I saw a replay of the goal, how hard I was trying to keep the ball low. You know, head down and over the ball, just like it says in all the coaching manuals. I connected well and there was too much pace on the ball for Jennings. We had finally managed to score and what happened next is part of Wembley folklore. I leapt high in the air and the rest of the players weren't slow to congratulate me. I was surrounded by them and everything was a blur. I was overcome with a mixture of emotion and exhaustion – that's all I can put it down to.

I can appreciate it all looked very dramatic at the time. You don't always see someone score and it's his last contribution. In my case, I was happy to give way to Mick Lambert. To my mind that's what the substitute was for. Had we used our sub beforehand I would have carried on, no question. I wouldn't have left my team with 10 men. I might have been groggy for a couple of minutes but I'd have got on with it for the final few minutes and seen it through. As it was, though, we had our 12th man ready and willing, so I was fine about coming off when I did. One more thing – it was far more nerve-racking sitting on the touchline waiting for the referee to blow the final whistle than it would have been if I'd stayed on the pitch. I joked afterwards that I had an arrangement to let Mick on because he was having his testimonial game on the Monday at Portman Road and he had promised me a few bob.

There was one near thing, when Alan Sunderland was through and Paul Cooper was off his line very quickly to dive at his feet, but it would have been an injustice had they levelled to take it into extra time. As the referee blew to signal the end of the game it sunk in that I had created my own little bit of history, an achievement to last for ever and something I simply wouldn't have thought possible a few years earlier. Before we went up to collect the cup I made a beeline for physio Tommy Eggleston because he had my false teeth. I had worn them right up until we were introduced to HRH Princess Alexandra before the game and then gave them to Tommy for safe keeping. I usually didn't bother and just left them in the dressing room but it was a very special occasion and I wanted to look my best.

WINNING THE FA CUP was massive for me but it was the same for the club and the manager. We had been there or thereabouts in the quest for major honours but you don't get remembered for coming close, only for winning. We were putting a trophy – not just any trophy, the FA Cup – in the boardroom and as a winning manager Bobby Robson's reputation couldn't have been better. It was all about having something to show for all the hard work that had been put in by him, his staff and the players. Another important factor was that I was a local lad, a supporter turned player. Nowadays you get players of different nationalities in the English game and no one will ever convince me that they have the same feeling for a club that someone born and raised in the area has.

It was an amazing 24 hours or so – the banquet in London, the journey home to Ipswich the next day and the open-top bus ride through the streets lined with thousands of supporters. One long party, in a way, and we were all shattered by the time we made our way home after the civic reception. In the weeks and months to come it was pretty hectic as we took the cup to all corners of the county and I suddenly found myself in demand for personal appearances. I went out and about a fair bit with the trophy and I remember one particular occasion when I was booked to take it up to Leiston and let the pupils at a school there have a close-up look at it. On the way home to Ipswich I drove past my old school, Farlingaye, and on the spur of the moment decided to drop in unannounced. I went in with the cup in its big brown wooden cabinet and introduced myself, and it was amazing the effect it had. Lessons were abandoned as the headmaster called an assembly and the pupils were astonished to see what all the fuss was about.

The FA Cup was the star attraction at several events during the summer of 1978. It meant so much to so many people all over Suffolk, so you can imagine how proud I felt to have played my part in bringing it to Ipswich for the first time. The look on people's faces when they saw the trophy, and inevitably had their picture taken with it, made the achievement all the more worthwhile. Older people, some with tears in their eyes, were telling me they never, ever imagined the FA Cup would come to Ipswich and how grateful they were that it had happened in their lifetime. The club had won the League Championship, a fantastic achievement in itself, but that had been 16 years earlier and it wasn't as if Ipswich were used to winning major honours on a regular basis.

We were paid a bonus of £2,000 a man for reaching Wembley and another £2,000 for winning the FA Cup. Good money at the time but it was secondary, in terms of importance, to the glory. How do you put a price on an FA Cup winner's medal, which is something I will always cherish and never part with, unlike the shirt I was wearing when I scored the winning goal? A few years ago I donated it to be auctioned on behalf of a breast cancer charity and it raised £5,500. I had absolutely no regrets at giving it away to such a worthwhile cause. I actually wore two shirts at Wembley – long sleeves in the first half and short in the second. Afterwards I swapped the long-sleeved shirt with Liam Brady and I have since allowed Town to borrow it to put it on display at Portman Road.

Over the years people have asked if I still have the boots I was wearing at Wembley and they are shocked when I tell them the honest truth – they were thrown away and ended up in a bin. Hindsight is a wonderful thing and if I'd held on to them they might be worth a lot of money today. I didn't play a great deal of football the following season and one day Allan

Hunter came to me and asked if he could borrow my boots because one of his had split. I let him have them and that was the last I saw of them. Allan wore them until they were no good and chucked them out. I don't blame him in any way because he did nothing wrong. At the time it never even entered my head to hang on to them.

I'm not short of souvenirs. I have a print of me scoring the goal from a watercolour that an artist did and a pewter plate that carries all the signatures of the Town squad. We also received a souvenir from Wembley Stadium – a hand-made figure – and of course there's my medal. I also have my memories and in a way they are as priceless as the medal. Yes, it really did happen and nobody can take it away from me.

JOHN WARK
MIDFIELD/CENTRE-HALF 1974–84/1988-91/1991-97

BORN   4 August 1957, Glasgow
SIGNED   1 – 13 August 1974 from apprentice
2 – January 1988 from Liverpool; £100,000
3 – September 1991; free agent
IPSWICH CAREER (three spells) 679 games, 179 goals
HONOURS   FA Cup 1978; UEFA Cup 1981; Second Division
Championship 1992; First Division runner-up 1981, 1982; PFA Player of the
Year 1981; Ipswich Player of the Year 1989, 1990, 1992, 1994; 29 Scotland caps
LEFT   1 – Transferred to Liverpool, March 1984; £400,000
2 – Transferred to Middlesbrough, July 1990; £50,000
3 – Became club scout in 1997 then was chief scout of both
Portsmouth and Coventry

A product of the club's successful youth system, John was introduced to the
first team in 1975 as a central defender but it was as a high-scoring midfield
player that he became best known, no more so than in 1981 when his fellow
professionals bestowed on him the game's highest individual honour by
voting him the PFA Player of the Year. He scored 36 goals that season, 14 of
them in 12 games to help Ipswich win the UEFA Cup, and in his first full
season with Liverpool he even managed to score more goals than Ian Rush.
He also played in the 1982 World Cup finals in Spain, when he scored twice
in Scotland's 5-2 win over New Zealand. Second in the club's all-time
appearance chart and third highest goalscorer, he had three spells with
Ipswich and was still playing at the age of 39, after which he turned to scouting. Now works as a match-day corporate hospitality host at Portman Road.

Ipswich Town 5 v Aris Salonika 1

UEFA Cup first round, first leg
Wednesday 17 September 1980

Portman Road
Attendance 20,842

Ipswich set out on the road to European glory with a resounding victory
and it's the shape of things to come as John Wark takes the scoring honours

Teams

Bobby Robson	**Managers**	Michal Vigam
Paul Cooper	1	Pantziaras
George Burley	2	Mokalis
Mick Mills	3	Pallas
Frans Thijssen	4	Venos
Russell Osman	5	Firos
Terry Butcher	6	Kouis
John Wark	7	Zindros
Arnold Muhren	8	Balis
(Sub. Kevin O'Callaghan)		
Paul Mariner	9	Tsirimokos
		(Sub. Dramis)
Alan Brazil	10	Semertzidis
(Sub. Kevin Beattie)		
Eric Gates	11	Zelidis

Wark 13 pen, 15, 29 pen, 78 pen,	Goals	Pallas 48 pen
Mariner 61		

Referee: Antonio Garrido (Portugal)

THE 1980/81 SEASON IS widely acknowledged as the best in Ipswich Town's history and on a personal basis it was by far my most successful as an individual, so when it came to selecting my top game I knew it would have to be one from that campaign.

Supporters who were around at the time will recall how we were trying to complete an unprecedented treble of three major honours – the League Championship, the FA Cup and the UEFA Cup – but ultimately had to settle for only one. I say 'only' because we really did believe, as the season was drawing to an end, that we could complete a hat-trick of top prizes and to only end up with one was actually a disappointment.

Normally, to have won a top European competition would have been regarded as a fabulous achievement – and on reflection it undoubtedly was – but I think I speak for all the players from that era when I say it turned out to be something of an anti-climax that we had to settle for just the one trophy when we genuinely believed we could capture all three.

When I reflect on my playing career, the fact that we failed to complete the domestic double, and join an elite group of clubs to have done so, will always be one of the biggest disappointments. I honestly think I should have another two medals in my collection and nobody will ever convince me otherwise.

We were pipped by Aston Villa for the title and good luck to them. They topped the league after every side had played 42 games and no one can argue with that. But we beat them both home and away that season, as well as knocking them out of the FA Cup at the first hurdle, and we had only ourselves to blame that we didn't finish on top.

Villa were fortunate that they managed to avoid any serious injuries and were able to field virtually an unchanged side from one game to the next, so much so that they fielded just 14 players over the entire league programme. I remember thinking at the time that it must be some sort of record and I was surprised to learn that it merely equalled one that had stood for a few years.

I don't want this to sound like sour grapes. Villa had four points more than we did by the end of the 1980/81 season, so the league crown was rightly theirs and we had to settle for runners-up spot. It might mean something these days when the top four in the Premiership find their way into the following season's Champions League but back then finishing second was . . . well, we were absolutely gutted and there's no other way to put it.

In the FA Cup we reached the semi-finals and seriously under-performed against Manchester City at Villa Park. We were a better side than them – we knew it, they knew it and the league table confirmed it. We still had to go out and do the business, however, and for some reason we were well below our best. We couldn't find the rhythm that was our trademark. On another day, when we were firing on all cylinders, we would have swept City aside. It was 0-0 after 90 minutes and I have absolutely no doubt that we would have made the final had we been able to call it quits and come back another day. That wasn't an option, however. The FA had decided to introduce extra time as a means of hopefully avoiding a replay and it was just our luck – we had already lost Kevin Beattie to a broken arm – that we were the first club to suffer as a result. We went down 1-0 and when our league hopes also evaporated in the weeks to follow we were suddenly facing the prospect of perhaps ending up with zilch to show for our efforts over what turned out to be a marathon, 66-game season, only two of which I missed.

Had we also been able to rely on just 14 players in the 42-game league programme I am certain we would have won the title. But the additional workload of the FA Cup and, to a far greater extent, the UEFA Cup, put us under considerable extra strain and, in the end, it told. Key players were absent for long spells – George Burley missed half the season with a career-threatening knee injury – and in the final reckoning we used a total of 21 players, exactly 50 per cent more than Villa did.

In the end, much to our eternal relief, we did win the UEFA Cup and it is the very first of the 12 games we played in that season's tournament that I have nominated, not least because I scored four goals, including a hat-trick of penalties, which made it unique from my point of view. Indeed, I am told that only one other player in Ipswich Town's history, George Perrett, also converted three penalties in one game. It was back in October 1936, just a few months after the club turned professional, during an FA Cup second qualifying round tie against Lowestoft Town, so I can at least claim my place in the record books as the first to perform the feat in Europe.

WHEN THE DRAW WAS MADE for the UEFA Cup in 1980 I was probably the only member of the Ipswich squad who knew anything about our opponents. My mother-in-law at the time, Pepi Elmslie, was not only Greek but actually came from a small town near Salonika and I had been over the previous year for a holiday, when I met a large number of her relatives.

I visited the Aris stadium and even had to turn down a signing offer from the club. A few weeks before we flew out there I played for Scotland against England at Wembley. It was only my third senior cap and I scored my first international goal to put us ahead, although we later conceded three to lose the game 3-1. By what I can only call a very strange coincidence, the game was being shown on television in Greece while I was out there and once the local paper got to hear that I was in the area they sent a reporter and photographer to talk to me.

That was just the start, because when I was chatting to the journalist I saw two men, who looked very official as they were dressed in smart suits and carrying briefcases, and I wondered who they were. They introduced themselves as being from the football club and straight away asked if I would be interested in signing for them. They really took me by surprise. I explained that I was under contract at Ipswich and even if I did want to move, which I didn't at the time, it would be impossible. It was a weird situation, to be honest, and when the draw paired us with Aris it was a massive coincidence.

The phone calls started that very same day. As well as having family and friends in the Salonika area, my mother-in-law also had a number of Greek friends based in Colchester and they made it known they would be coming along to the first game. There were quite a lot of Greeks in the crowd that night and they saw a very lively first half that included three goals, a sending off and five bookings. From their point of view it couldn't have been much fun as they saw their team go in at half-time trailing 3-0 and having been reduced to 10 men.

We were naturally keen to make a flying start but what occurred exceeded even our wildest expectations. We were not rookies in terms of European experience and we knew the value of building up a decent first-leg lead, although there had been times when a 3-0 advantage had not proved to be enough and on other occasions a slender one-goal lead had enabled us to progress. I think we had always felt we could make more of an impact in Europe than we had done in previous seasons but there was no way we were thinking 'We're going to win it' when we kicked off against Aris. For a start, we knew it would be tough over there, which made it all the more important that we established a decent lead from the first game.

We should have known what to expect when Eric Gates was crudely upended inside the first 20 seconds but if they thought that would be the end of Gatesy they were to be proved wrong several times over. He took quite a lot of punishment in games and although he kept going back for more he was also entitled to some protection from the referee. The same player who had fouled him soon after the kick-off did it again in the 13th minute and because it was inside the area we had a penalty. I don't want it to sound as if I was arrogant but as soon as a referee pointed to the spot I used to think to myself 'Goal' because I was so confident of scoring.

I stepped up and placed the ball on the spot before striking it low to the keeper's right. I caught it well and it's true that players know the split second the ball leaves their boot whether or not it's going to be successful. The contact was good and I have always maintained that if the player taking the penalty strikes the ball properly the goalkeeper should have absolutely no chance of stopping it.

The crowd were still singing when we extended our lead. The keeper didn't hold a cross from Mick Mills and as I chested the ball down there were five or six players between me and the goal. But I spotted a narrow gap and managed to side-foot the ball through it into the net for what I considered to be quite a good goal. With less than half an hour on the clock we were 3-0 ahead, another foul on Gatesy inside the area earning us a second penalty. This time I struck the ball high to the keeper's right and although he dived in the right direction there was no way he could reach it.

Before the break Aris were down to 10 men, another foul on Gatesy proving costly, but they managed to reduce the leeway within three minutes of the restart. It was another penalty but to be honest it was pretty soft. Terry Butcher was punished for what looked a perfectly fair tackle and although we protested we maybe didn't do so as strongly as we would have done had the game been more evenly balanced. To be fair to the lad who took the penalty he hit it well and Paul Cooper, who had a bit of a reputation for saving penalties, had no chance on that occasion. For a time Aris knocked the ball around quite well and it made me wonder how they might have coped had they adopted that attitude right from the start, rather than being as cynical as they were with what could only be called bully-boy tactics.

We were not content to sit on a 3-1 lead and just past the hour mark we scored what most people believed was the best goal on the night. Once again Gatesy was involved and George Burley raced on to his pass before crossing for Paul Mariner to find the net with a tremendous finish. We were awarded our final penalty with about 12 minutes left and, surprise, surprise, it came about as a result of a foul on Gatesy, who had his legs taken away as he was about to control a pass from Kevin O'Callaghan.

As I stepped up to place the ball I was having a good think about what to do. I had never been in that position before – very few players ever are – and having hit my first two to the keeper's right I was wondering what might be going through his mind. My intention was to go for the same side, mainly because I felt the keeper would be expecting me to change, but I actually changed my mind as I ran up to take the kick. That is the cardinal sin of penalty-taking but on this occasion I managed to get away with it. The ball flew high to the keeper's left and he had no hope of getting any-where near it. I was very relieved because the few penalties I did miss as an Ipswich player were all as a result of me changing my mind but on that occasion I not only managed to score but I also wrong-footed the keeper, who was clearly expecting me to aim for the other side of the goal.

That was the end of the scoring but while we were delighted to have forged a 5-1 lead we were taking nothing for granted – not with a second game still to play. The Aris players were booed off by the Portman Road crowd and were clearly incensed at what had happened, so much so that they were muttering things to us that, roughly translated, meant 'Wait until you come to our place'. After I got changed I went to the players' lounge and met up with my Greek relatives and friends, who were not happy bunnies I think it would be fair to say.

ON THE NIGHT WE WERE far too good for Aris. They were clearly of the view that they could frustrate us but to be honest the way they went about it was suicidal. They were reckless with their challenges, which cost them three penalties and a red card, and they could have no complaints that the referee punished them. They tried to accuse Gatesy of diving for the penalties but that was rubbish. There might have been a few occasions when Gatesy won a penalty that was, shall we say, dubious – but not that night. They were all clear-cut and they weren't the first side to realise how tricky a customer Gatesy was to play against. I've watched the video and they wiped him out three times inside the area, simple as that.

Bobby Robson would encourage us to get the ball into Gatesy's feet as often as possible. He was short, stocky and had a low centre of gravity, which made it quite easy for him to 'turn' defenders. Basically he would shape as if to go one way and then change direction at the very last second, virtually forcing players to foul him. Even if he had a defender breathing down his neck we were told to feed the ball into him at every opportunity, because if he didn't get away from his marker and get in a shot he would invariably be brought down.

Gatesy would win them and I would put them away – it was a useful partnership that worked for Ipswich on numerous occasions. He was clever in as much that he would almost invite the challenge and it was well within the rules of the game. That night I took a great deal of satisfaction from converting three penalties because each finish was pretty clinical and the keeper wasn't even close to getting near any of them. It can be a battle of wits between the keeper and the player taking a penalty but I just liked to get hold of the ball, put it on the spot and avoid all eye contact with the keeper. I always believed that if I struck the ball properly I would score and, as I've said, when I missed it was usually down to me changing my mind and not getting enough power behind my kick.

It was yet another memorable European night at Portman Road and we had a few over the years. We always looked forward to playing under the lights because it created a special atmosphere. To be blunt about it, we didn't just beat teams, we used to dish out quite a few hammerings, as even Barcelona found out. My match-day routine was always the same – we would not train on the morning of the game, but maybe have a loosening-up session and some players did nothing more strenuous than have a nice long bath. I'd have a light lunch and then head home, where I would usually manage a kip from about 1pm to 4pm or 5pm, then I would get changed and be at the ground by 6pm.

Kenny Dalglish taught me the value of a good sleep. When I roomed with him on Scotland trips I was a good few years younger than him and I'd be ready to watch a late-night movie or some other programme when he would announce 'Right, Warky, time for us to get to sleep'. Kenny had his routine – he would ask me to pull the curtains, switch the telly off and take the phone off the hook. To be honest I'd have rather stayed awake for another couple of hours, but Kenny always got his own way and in fairness to him, as I got older I have to say I began to realise how right he was to make the most of his sleep. Maybe I owe him a huge debt of gratitude, in fact, because I didn't hang up my boots until my 40th year and even after I'd celebrated my 50th birthday I was still enjoying my Sunday morning games.

THAT IPSWICH TEAM IN 1980/81 was as good as any – and I'm not just talking about England but Europe too. In fact, I doubt if there was a better club side anywhere in the world that season. I realise that is some statement but I really do believe it. We were a perfect blend and what was strange about my role, considering the number of goals I scored, was that I was actually intended to be the most defensive of the four midfielders. We had a diamond system before anyone had even thought of calling it that – me at one end, Gatesy at the other, and the two Dutchmen, Arnold Muhren and Frans Thijssen, on the left and right.

I was brought up as a defender and I played at the back, as well as in midfield, as a youngster and in my first few Ipswich first team games. It was an instinctive thing the way I could win the ball in front of my own back four and then spread the play to either wing, at which I point I would generally get on my bike and head towards the other end of the pitch. Bobby Robson called me a box to box player and that was an accurate description, I suppose. I always felt that if I could get near to, or in, the opposition box I would have a good chance of scoring but I tried not to get there too soon. I would look to time my runs and get on the end of crosses, clearances and knock-downs, and I never had a season where I was more successful than in 1980-81.

I have to confess, though, that even when I started with four goals against Aris I wasn't thinking of equalling a long-standing European record, but that's exactly what I had done by the time we won the trophy in Amsterdam eight months later. I had netted 14 times in 12 games and that tally was on a par with Jose Altafini of AC Milan when he helped the Italian giants to win the European Cup in 1963, knocking Ipswich out in the very first round.

Mind you, every time I think about that UEFA Cup victory I think of the away leg against Aris, where we survived a massive scare. I suppose it was a bit like Bristol Rovers in the FA Cup in 1978 in that we were walking a bit of a tightrope. The atmosphere in Salonika was very hostile, not just on the day of the game but throughout our stay. We had to have an armed bodyguard because it was known as bandit country and the local authorities were taking no chances. We even had Aris supporters trying to disrupt our training – about 200 of them gatecrashed the session – and in the game itself we had what is known in the business as a 'mare.

We heard that the local fans had been brainwashed into thinking Ipswich had bribed the referee at Portman Road, which explained why Aris had conceded three penalties and had a man sent off. The Greek television channels had apparently gone overboard, too, in trying to give the impression that the referee was corrupt and with the local newspapers also jumping on the bandwagon it certainly had the desired effect of stoking up the atmosphere against us.

With 65 minutes on the clock we were trailing 3-0. One more goal to them and we were out. You could maybe say we were a bit too casual in our approach, but it was partly due to the fact that we were being ultra cautious in case we gave the referee an excuse to start waving his red card about. And to be fair, Aris played far better than they had looked capable of in the first game but they were getting away with murder. They were spitting in our faces and generally trying to intimidate us, and neither the referee nor his two linesmen were doing anything to prevent them. They scored after only four minutes, although we were adamant the ball had not crossed the line. It would have taken a brave referee to disallow it. The pitch was hard and bumpy, with areas completely without grass, and I'm serious when I say I've played on better in the Ipswich and District Licensed Trades League.

They also had 40,000 supporters almost baying for blood, so we had quite a lot on our plate. Bobby Robson knew what to expect. He told us beforehand that he thought they would try every trick in the book. He said they would attempt to win free-kicks and penalties in key areas, and he told us to be careful we did not get dragged down to their level. He reminded us how their loss of discipline had proved so costly to them in the first game and he didn't want us to fall into the same trap over there.

The game was played in the afternoon, not the evening, and at 3-0 we were starting to fear the worst, thinking we might be on our way out of the competition. Fortunately, though, Gatesy popped up with a shot and there was no way it could have been disputed. That meant Aris would have to score two more to force extra time, which might have been possible with about 17 minutes left to play except that they seemed to sense it was too high a mountain to climb.

The unfriendly atmosphere continued afterwards when we returned to the dressing rooms and discovered there was no hot water for baths and showers. Instead we put our tracksuits on and, knowing we had all the facilities we needed back at the hotel, we made a beeline for the bus. An angry mob of supporters was waiting just outside the area where the bus was parked and as it moved off a brick came flying through a window where George Burley was sitting. That was the signal for everyone to get down on the floor until we had gathered sufficient speed to shake off the hooligans.

From my point of view that first game against Aris shines out because of the fact that I scored four of our goals, including the three penalties, but there were so many highlights in that unforgettable season. Winning the

UEFA Cup was clearly the main one for the club and I really began to think in terms of us going all the way when we went over to St Etienne and completely outclassed them. My reasoning was that if we could beat such a good team – Michel Platini was their star man – so convincingly in their own back yard we could surely beat anyone.

From an individual point of view I was also named as the PFA Player of the Year and that was a tremendous accolade. Because it was my fellow professionals at clubs up and down the country who cast their votes, it meant an awful lot to me. I was also voted European Young Player of the Year in a poll run by an Italian magazine but I often wonder if any of the individual honours, or indeed the UEFA Cup winner's medal I cherish, would have come my way if we had not bulldozed Aris in the very first game of our European adventure.

ALAN BRAZIL
STRIKER 1977–1983

BORN 15 June 1959, Glasgow
SIGNED 30 May 1977 from apprentice
IPSWICH CAREER 210 games, 80 goals
HONOURS UEFA Cup 1981; First Division runner-up 1981, 1982; Ipswich Player of the Year 1981; 13 Scotland caps
LEFT Transferred to Tottenham, 15 March 1983; £450,000

Alan was spotted by Scottish scout George Findlay, who was also responsible for taking fellow international stars George Burley and John Wark to Ipswich, and he was snapped up from under the noses of his boyhood favourites, Celtic. He was a prolific marksman for Celtic Boys' Club, whose better players were invariably taken to Parkhead, but he never regretted his decision to head south of the border. The club's FA Cup success in 1978 came too soon for him but he was a key member of the UEFA Cup-winning side of 1981 and he was Town's 28-goal top scorer the following year, when Ipswich finished runners-up in the First Division for the second successive season. After Tottenham he went on to play for Manchester United, Coventry and QPR before having to retire prematurely due to a back injury. He pursued a media career and worked for the BBC, ITV and Sky Sports before joining talkSPORT, where he currently presents the award-winning flagship breakfast show.

Ipswich Town 5 v Southampton 2

First Division
Tuesday 16 February 1982

Portman Road
Attendance 20,264

*Brazil becomes the first player in Ipswich's history to score five goals in a
league game as he single-handedly sees off the First Division leaders with a
devastating display of top-class finishing*

Teams

	Managers	
Bobby Robson	**Managers**	Lawrie McMenemy
Paul Cooper	1	Ivan Katalinic
George Burley	2	Ivan Golac
		(Sub. George Lawrence)
Steve McCall	3	Nick Holmes
Mick Mills	4	Graham Baker
Russell Osman	5	Chris Nicholl
Kevin Steggles	6	Malcolm Waldron
John Wark	7	Kevin Keegan
Arnold Muhren	8	Mick Channon
Mich D'Avray	9	David Puckett
Alan Brazil	10	David Armstrong
Eric Gates	11	Alan Ball
Brazil 14, 17, 19, 69, 86	Goals	Puckett 43, Keegan 76

Referee: Jeff Bray (Hinckley)

I MAY HAVE PLAYED FOR 'bigger' clubs than Ipswich in Tottenham Hotspur and Manchester United but everyone who has ever met me – and especially regular listeners to my show on talkSPORT – will know that I am Town through and through. So much so, in fact, that as I reflect on my career it is the goals I scored for Ipswich against both Spurs and United, rather than those I netted for those two clubs, that I tend to remember. Of course, nothing comes even close to the night I bagged all five against Southampton, which still stands as a club record. I know the great Ray Crawford scored five in the European Cup defeat of Floriana back in 1962 but no one else can match my feat of scoring five in a league game – and a top-flight one at that. From a purely selfish standpoint, I would love the record to last for ever and even if it doesn't it will be interesting to see who, and when, somebody does manage to equal or even beat it.

I was a part of so many fabulous team performances at Ipswich in the early 80s that it might have been difficult to choose one ahead of all the rest, but because of my five goals the Southampton game is head and shoulders above them all as far as I am concerned. I scored a hat-trick – and this is almost unbelievable – in the space of just five minutes. I remember thinking 'This must be about as good as it gets' but come the final whistle, by which time I had added another two, I really was on cloud nine.

What will probably surprise you, however, is that after getting changed and doing a couple of interviews – the media interest in football back then was nothing like as intense as it is today – I jumped in my car and drove home. I remember giving one of the local reporters a pretty naff quote, something about expecting to see pigs flying across Portman Road when I emerged from the dressing room, but it really was low key compared to how I think the media would treat the same story today. There was no Sky Sports or Setanta back then, of course.

I have, shall we say, a certain reputation these days because of my fondness for the good things in life, hence the bon viveur reference in the title of my first book, *There's An Awful Lot of Bubbly in Brazil*, but I could never have been accused of overdoing the celebrations following the game against Southampton. To be honest, if I was in any way light-headed it was because

I couldn't really believe what I had done, and all the way home I was in a state of disbelief. As I walked in the door, News at Ten was on and up flashed a picture of me as they reported on what was a major sports story at the time.

My wife, Jill, to whom I was married just a few weeks earlier, actually missed the game. She only decided about an hour beforehand that she wouldn't go that night and gave her ticket to a friend. She switched on the radio to hear how we were getting on and by that time I had already scored twice. Needless to say, as the goals continued to fly in, she regretted her decision more and more. Oddly enough, it was the first home game she had missed since we had met and started going out a couple of years earlier. She was absolutely gutted at missing out on my special moment and even as I joked that I would get another five next time, just for her, we both knew it was extremely unlikely to happen again.

From a personal point of view, I was in good form going into the Southampton game, with eight goals in my previous 10 appearances, a combination of league, FA Cup and League Cup fixtures. More importantly, though, it was not the best of times for the club as we had slipped from top place in the First Division and also gone out of the other two competitions within the space of a few days. We were actually down in seventh place in the table, albeit with several games in hand, while Southampton were top of the pile, as we approached the game. Just three days earlier we had been on the wrong end of an FA Cup giant-killing act at Shrewsbury and that had come just four days after we were KO'd at the semi-final stage of the League Cup by Liverpool, who went on to retain the trophy they had won the previous year. We had also lost 4-0 at Anfield and, hard to believe these days, Notts County had turned us over 3-1 at Portman Road, so we had surrendered a number of valuable league points.

Some people – supporters and press, definitely not the players – were actually thinking in terms of Southampton collecting at least a point from the game. Lawrie McMenemy's side were on a terrific run, which had taken them two points clear of Manchester United at the top of the league and, apart from our indifferent form, we were minus three very influential players in defender Terry Butcher, midfielder Frans Thijssen and striker Paul Mariner, in a sense the backbone of our team, and that went a long way to explaining our disappointing run of results.

Typically, though, none of that seemed to count for anything on the night. In fact, PM's replacement, Mich D'Avray, who was making only his third league start for the club, had a part in several of the goals. He was probably relishing a rare opportunity because being South African, and with the rules as they were at the time, he could only play when one of the two Dutch players was absent. My first goal was in the 14th minute and came about as a result of Kevin Steggles, who was in for big Butch, putting in a terrific long ball that Mich headed over Saints' defender Ivan Golac. One of the key things about playing up front is to be able to read a situation and know what your fellow striker is going to do, and that enabled me to get on the ball and finish. Three minutes later we were 2-0 ahead as Mich challenged their keeper and again I anticipated what was going to happen and swept the loose ball into an empty net. I completed my hat-trick when I ran on to Kevin Steggles' through ball and outpaced Nick Holmes before planting a firm shot into the bottom corner of the net.

Saints pulled one back just before half-time but we made it 4-1 in the 69th minute when Mick Mills and Mich D'Avray worked a good move between them to set me up and I brushed off a challenge from Holmes to run on and score. Kevin Keegan netted Saints' second goal and four minutes from the end I scored my fifth after an excellent move that involved Arnold Muhren and, yet again, Mich D'Avray, although it was Eric Gates' pass that finally left me in the clear to stick the ball away. I remember running towards the North Stand, where the supporters were going mad, and there's a famous picture that appeared in the match programme for the next game of me jumping over one of the advertising boards. It actually looks as if I am walking on air, which is exactly how I felt at the time.

It sounds like a bit of a whitewash but Saints were not at the top of the First Division for nothing and I remember a couple of goal-line clearances by Mick Mills and Russell Osman or it might have been a lot closer. They were a very good side, packed with experience, and they went into the game having lost just one of their previous 13. At the final whistle I went to get hold of the match ball and although I still have it among my souvenirs to this day, it isn't actually what it seems. Unfortunately, the one I have is the second ball that was used that night after the first was cleared over the roof of what was then known as Churchmans and is now the Greene King Stand. Normally the ball would be retrieved pretty quickly but on that occasion somebody must have got hold of it and kept it because it was never recovered, despite me making a bit of a plea a couple of days later via the local paper. And, would you believe, I had already scored four times before the switch, so the ball I have only went into the Saints' net once.

THE VERY NEXT DAY I was ferried across to Newmarket by *The Sun* newspaper and had my picture taken with one of the greatest racehorses of all time, Shergar, who had won the previous year's Derby by a record distance of 10 lengths. *The Sun* knew I was a big racing fan and to be honest I wasn't going to miss a chance like that. There was just one problem – the horse's trainer, Michael Stoute, apparently knew nothing about it and he was none too pleased. Naturally, I assumed everything had been arranged and I ended up writing him a letter to explain that and to apologise for any inconvenience I had caused. I had a game of golf later that day with Paul Mariner and was disappointed that I didn't manage a hole in one.

No two ways about it – 1982 was a very good year for me with a number of other highlights over and above that five-goal display. One that meant a great deal to me was being voted Player of the Year by the Ipswich supporters – when I looked on the trophy and saw all the great names that had won it in previous years it made me realise what an accolade it was. It didn't end there, however, because the club sponsors, Pioneer, and the executive box holders also presented me with their own Player of the Year awards, which made it a clean sweep of the individual honours. I also picked up a cheque for £1,000 and a colour television from the Sunday People newspaper for being the top striker based on the marks handed out by their reporters over the course of the season. There was also a chance that I would follow my pal – even if he supports the wrong half of the Old Firm – John Wark as the PFA Player of the Year, which is probably the highest individual award in the game alongside the journalists' Footballer of the Year award. I was short-listed for it, and also in the Young Player of the Year category, but the eventual winners were Kevin Keegan and Steve Moran – both, ironically enough, Southampton players.

Talking of coincidences, it was also in 1982 that I recorded what I consider to be the only career highlight that comes anywhere near my achievement of scoring five goals in a league game. It was another 5-2 game but this time for Scotland against New Zealand in the World Cup finals over in Spain. I didn't score – Warky got two – but the reason it meant so much was that the game was played on my 23rd birthday and I played alongside the one and only Kenny Dalglish, my boyhood idol. When I was a youngster growing up in Glasgow, my bedroom wall was plastered with pictures of Kenny and I was a regular on the terraces at Parkhead as he inspired Celtic to one major honour after another. It really was the stuff of dreams to be playing in the World Cup as a team-mate of his, something that had never really crossed my mind, say, 10 years earlier when he was already an established star and I was a kid just dreaming of becoming a professional.

I'd have loved to have played in the next World Cup game against Brazil but the simple truth is that I was cream-crackered. The 90-degree heat on the Costa del Sol was fine for getting a tan but it was murder trying to play football in it. Being of fair complexion – and having had asthmatic problems as a youngster – I suffered more than most, although Gordon Strachan was also struggling. We said at half-time that we would carry on for another 10 to 15 minutes but I was literally seeing double by then. I came off and when I weighed myself I discovered I had lost 10 pounds. Then some joker decided I should be one of the players – John Robertson, the Nottingham Forest winger, was the other – to supply a urine sample. There was no way I could oblige. FIFA rules said I should have been kept at the stadium for up to 16 hours but they decided to allow me to return to the team hotel with orders to report back to the stadium the following day at 1pm. But that was against the rules and the test was declared invalid. After what had happened four years earlier in Argentina, when Willie Johnston was sent home because they found traces of a banned substance, I found myself at the centre of another Scottish football controversy, although I did feature in our last game against the Soviet Union.

LOOKING BACK, THE 1981/82 season started as a bit of a non-event for me. I had a trapped nerve in my left foot and I required painkilling injections to get through games. Eventually, though, surgery was the only answer and I was delighted to return after missing just six games. But I also might have departed Ipswich before my five-goal display against Southampton. I actually submitted a written transfer request a few months earlier, but after a chat with Bobby Robson, who said there was no way he would have agreed to it, I decided to withdraw it.

Why did I want to get away? It was because of a bust-up with the first team coach, Bobby Ferguson. We were playing at Stoke and he kept barking at me to pull wide on to the left wing. I'll be honest – I pretended not to hear him, because I was no winger. We lost the game 2-0 and I was having a shower when Bobby joined me, fully clothed, to have a go and ask why I had ignored his instructions. As far as I was concerned it was the final straw and the time had come to bring matters to a head. I had not always seen eye to eye with Fergie and I thought a parting of the ways might be the best solution. In the end, though, not only did Bobby Robson talk me round, but when he went off to take charge of England a few months later, and Fergie succeeded him, I agreed a new five-year contract to stay at Portman Road.

But I soon regretted that decision as players began to leave the club without being adequately replaced. Arnold Muhren was first to go, then Mick Mills, and I could see it all falling apart. Fergie and I never really got along. I felt he was a bully and I know several others who shared that view. Even when I attended the ex-players' reunion dinner in March 2008 he had a go and accused me of writing lies in my book. It was quite confrontational and also embarrassing, plus it was 25 years after we had parted company and I could have done without it. The club had financial problems when they sold me to Tottenham in 1983 and while I knew it was the right thing to do, in a way it broke my heart to leave. The good times far outweighed the bad in my years with Ipswich. I went there as a boy and going back to my youth team days, I remember scoring four goals in each of four successive games in the same month. I was also named the South East Counties League Player of the Year, an honour previously won by such household names as Bobby Moore and Jimmy Greaves, and getting into the Scotland youth team eventually led to me winning caps at under-23 and senior levels.

We were a top, top side in the 1980-81 season, when I played in 58 of our 66 games at home and in Europe, scoring 18 goals. We won the UEFA Cup and I never missed a game in that competition, although I only got one goal. In my view we were such a good side that season that we would have won the European Cup if we had been in it and I have some strong evidence to back up that claim. Aston Villa won the Championship but we beat them twice and also knocked them out of the FA Cup – and the following year they were European champions. In my view, we were only runners-up to Villa because we had such a heavy workload and our squad lacked the depth to cope with injuries. Villa were helped by the fact that they were only chasing success on one front and fielded virtually the same side week in, week out. We also finished second in 1982, to Liverpool, but after Bobby Robson's departure I'm afraid we went downhill pretty rapidly and it made sense for me to depart when I did.

I won another UEFA Cup winner's medal with Spurs, but believe it or not I don't really count it. I also scored in our 5-0 win over Arsenal in a North London derby at White Hart Lane, but when I was given the chance to move on to Manchester United in the summer of 1984 I jumped at it. Ron Atkinson was the manager at the time and he had tried to get me from Ipswich without success. He paid £625,000, which was a huge sum of money at the time, and I was desperate to succeed at Old Trafford. United had money in the bank from the sale of Ray Wilkins to AC Milan and Big Ron went on a spending spree in a bid to put a halt to the Merseyside monopoly of the domestic scene. He also brought in Gordon Strachan and Jesper Olsen, two wide men, but I was the type who relied on service and to get the very best out of me I had to play off a target man, like I had done so successfully with Paul Mariner at Ipswich.

It didn't work out at United, where I even had to contend with supporters spitting at me. You wouldn't have treated a dog the way Big Ron treated me, either. He told me he was doing a swap deal with Coventry that would bring Terry Gibson to United, and when I told him to forget it he put the boot in. He said I would rot in the reserves and the club clearly held the upper hand. The writing was on the wall as I made just one start in the 1985-86 season and in the end I had no choice but to move. I was, quite literally, sent to Coventry in January 1986, although I maintain I did well to score 12 times in my 24 starts for United, especially as the system we played didn't really suit me. In the summer of 1986 I was on the move again, this time to Queen's Park Rangers, to play for one of the nicest guys in the game, Jim Smith.

Sadly, I only managed four games for QPR before I was forced to call it a day. I was only 27 and I should have been at my peak. Instead, my career was over. I had never felt 100 per cent at Tottenham and Manchester United, but I was never able to get to the root of the problem, and it was only when I got to Coventry that I realised it was my back. I was amazed that my medical at QPR comprised little more than being asked to touch my toes – I was expecting a far more thorough examination – and, sure enough, the back problem soon flared up to the extent that I had no choice but to retire. I had a few business interests before I settled down to become a publican in Ipswich, but that wasn't the success I wanted it to be and I was close to bankruptcy, although I eventually paid out hundreds of thousands of pounds to my creditors.

MY MEDIA CAREER STARTED modestly with BBC Radio Suffolk and the local paper before I started to spread my wings and appeared all over the place, including Anglia TV. I used to think nothing of getting up in what seemed like the middle of the night to drive to London for an appearance on GMTV, and after stints on Eurosport and Radio 5Live I eventually landed a deal with Sky Sports to be the main co-commentator on their coverage of The Football League. In 1999 I made the switch back to radio with talkSPORT and I love my role presenting the breakfast show from

6am to 10am. I do it from Monday to Thursday, then on Saturday I am involved in the live match coverage. It might sound like a cushy number, but talking virtually non-stop for four hours wouldn't suit everyone and it often leaves me mentally shattered, which is why I like to unwind with a glass or two of decent wine.

It's been a bit of a rollercoaster ride at talkSPORT these past nine years. I'm not denying I have a great lifestyle most of the time and I am recognised far more now than I ever was in my playing days. But a lot of people ask me how I am able to cope, and I know it's not everyone who could handle it. My philosophy has always been the same – to enjoy life to the max – and I have always subscribed to the view that we are only here for a visit, and that we're also a long time dead. I vowed a long time ago that I would not let things get me down, even the threat of bankruptcy when my pub business collapsed and being sacked by talkSPORT. I have twice survived the axe, which is probably one of the greatest achievements of my life.

The first time it happened was as a result of missing the show that followed a three-day stint at the Cheltenham Festival. I knew I was in trouble and when I arrived home Jill, having opened the letter, greeted me with the words "You've lost your job." My response, my way of dealing with it, was to head off abroad on a skiing trip with my three daughters and while I was away there was such an outcry from the listeners that the station agreed to take me back. Unfortunately, it happened again and this time I was reinstated after I agreed to hand over a £5,000 fine if I missed any shows in the future. Kelvin MacKenzie, who is no longer at the station, was the man who sacked me, but he never did it face to face. On each occasion he either sent a letter to my home or he asked Mike Parry to fire me. He had previously been editor of *The Sun* and had a reputation as a disciplinarian, although I would have to say I found him to be a bit of a bully, which is a different thing altogether. The reason he flipped was that he couldn't handle me, nor could he hack the way I chose to live my life.

I would never try to claim that I have a model lifestyle, but I'm not daft either and if I overdo things one week I will make sure I compensate the next. I also make sure I do my homework. I spend most of my time talking about football, but I'm not a pundit in the way that Andy Gray, Alan Hansen and Alan Shearer are. Yes, I keep up to date with what's happening in the game, but I don't only read the back pages. Every day I read a couple of national papers all the way through and last thing at night I flick through the Ceefax and Teletext pages so that I know what's going on in the world. When I was at school in Glasgow – my home was very close to Hampden

Park – I definitely under-achieved because I was obsessed with football, but these days I have a good all-round knowledge and I am in no way one-dimensional.

I still live close to Ipswich but I also have an apartment in London, otherwise I couldn't cope with the early starts. My back problem remains – the medical term is degenerative changes in the spine – and if I accept an invitation to take part, say, in a charity golf tournament it usually means I've had it for the next four days or so.

Basically, the two bottom discs in my spine are virtually worn out and when bone rubs against bone the pain can be unbearable. I've had all sorts of treatment, including injections and acupuncture, but I've had to learn to live with it. I don't let it get me down – I'm generally happy and the one thing I regard as mega important is that my family are happy, healthy and well looked after.

I enjoy my football but nobody will ever convince me that the game today is any better than when I played. Everything is different – the pitches don't compare with the mud-heaps we often had to play on, while the equipment, the balls and the boots, are so much lighter, but in my view we are just kidding ourselves if we think the game itself is any better. I would think about three quarters of the goals I scored came when I was one on one with the opposition goalkeeper, and it amazes me that I see so few goals like that in the Premiership. Goalkeepers only have one chance and as soon as they make their move I am puzzled why so few players have the ability to drop their shoulder and go round them. I had that ability as a kid and I still had it long after I scored my first goal for Ipswich past the great Peter Shilton, who was probably the best goalkeeper in the world at the time.

JASON DOZZELL
MIDFIELD/STRIKER 1984-1993/1997

BORN 9 December 1967, Ipswich
SIGNED 12 December 1984
IPSWICH CAREER 416 games, 73 goals
HONOURS Second Division Championship 1991-92; 9 England Under-21 caps; England B international
LEFT 1 - Transferred to Tottenham Hotspur, 1 August 1993, £1.9 million
2 - released after short-term stay; joined Northampton Town

Jason earned himself a coveted place in the record books when he became the youngest-ever goalscorer in the top flight of English football. He was just 16 years and 57 days old when he netted for Ipswich against Coventry and he went on to feature in the club's all-time top ten appearance makers and goalscorers before his big-money move to Tottenham, which in turn led to him being on the fringe of senior international honours. After four years at White Hart Lane and a free agent, he returned to Portman Road in the hope of earning himself a contract but manager George Burley instead decided not to take up the option and Jason joined Northampton before finishing his senior career with Colchester.

Ipswich Town 3 v Coventry City 1

First Division
Saturday 4 February 1984

Portman Road
Attendance 13,406

*Jason rewrites the record books as he becomes the youngest-ever
goalscorer in the English top flight at the age of 16 years and 57 days*

Teams

Bobby Ferguson	Managers	Bobby Gould
Paul Cooper	1	Raddy Avramovic
George Burley	2	Peter Hormantschuk
		(Sub. John Hendrie)
Steve McCall	3	Brian Roberts
Trevor Putney	4	Ashley Grimes
Russell Osman	5	Trevor Peake
Terry Butcher	6	Ian Butterworth
John Wark	7	Dave Bennett
Mark Brennan	8	Terry Gibson
Paul Mariner	9	Nicky Platnauer
Eric Gates	10	Gerry Daly
(Sub. Jason Dozzell)		
Kevin O'Callaghan	11	Graham Withey
Mariner 13, Brennan 16, Dozzell 89	Goals	Gibson 71

Referee: Ken Salmon (Southgate)

To SAY I WAS TAKEN aback at the speed of my progress in football would be the understatement of the century. Even now, having turned 40, my story takes a bit of believing and I can still hardly credit what happened to me in such a short space of time. It would be no exaggeration to say that it seemed one minute I was a supporter standing on the terracing behind the goal and the next I was out there on the Portman Road pitch, playing for the club I had followed for years. Like every other young Town fan, I desperately wanted to play for the club but I knew the difference between ambition and reality, so it was never a case of expecting it to happen and definitely not while I was still at school.

The path to stardom for most youngsters usually involves a two-year apprenticeship with the academy, during which they look to do enough to be taken on as professionals when they reach the age of 18. But even then it's just a step along the way and no guarantee of becoming a first team regular. The game is full of examples of young guys turning pro but then failing to make the grade and being released. There was nothing even the slightest bit conventional about my own situation – it was a bit like living a dream to find myself involved with the first team squad. Suddenly I was in the dressing room alongside people I idolised – Terry Butcher, John Wark, Paul Mariner and others – and I can't deny I found it all a bit daunting.

This takes a bit of believing, but I was so shy and nervous back then that when I used to go into the club I would go and hide in the boiler room alongside all the kit that was hanging up to dry after being washed in the laundry next door. There would be row upon row of training and match gear so it was easy to kill a few minutes in there without being spotted. I was in there on some occasions for as long as half an hour before I felt confident enough to go into the dressing room with the other guys. That went on for a few weeks until I felt properly at home and started to join in the banter and have conversations with the rest of the players.

You have to bear in mind that I was less than two months past my 16th birthday. Let's be honest, none of us know a great deal at such a tender age. I was both nervous and excited about being asked to play for the reserves, but I seemed to take it in my stride and scored five times in six appearances, two of which were as substitute. But being told I was going to be in the first team squad for the game against Coventry was an entirely different feeling. I was told the club had contacted my school about me having Thursday morning off so that I could go training at Portman Road with the senior players and that was the first time I realised something was up, although I had no idea what.

It was weird reporting for training with the first team lads and I felt even stranger when manager Bobby Ferguson pulled me to one side afterwards and told me I was going to be in the squad for the game against Coventry two days later. He probably knew there and then that he was going to put me on the bench – just the one substitute in those days – but he didn't let on to me. I guess he didn't want to let me know too soon in case I was a bundle of nerves for the next 48 hours or so. As far as I was concerned I was just going along for the ride. I was one of 16 players in the squad and I was one of the four who would not be taking any part. To be honest, when I looked around and saw so many well-known players, I actually wondered what I was doing there!

On the Saturday I reported in time for the pre-match meal at noon and I was still under the impression that I was there for the experience and nothing more. I was delighted to be involved but in my view there were another 15 guys there who were all way ahead of me and it never occurred to me that I would make the bench. Bobby told me just after 1pm, less than two hours before the kick-off, and I thought it was fantastic. Although I was a bit nervous I think the fact that I was so young meant that the scale of what was happening didn't really register. I have to confess that a lot of what was going on around me back then went over my head. The fact that Ipswich had been knocked out of the FA Cup at Shrewsbury the previous Saturday was probably relevant – the manager clearly wanted to freshen things up and maybe he felt that he didn't have too many options at his disposal.

I look back now and realise it was such a massive thing, not just because I was still a schoolboy but because I had been a supporter and to suddenly be pitched into a first team fixture seemed too good to be true. I had been in the Junior Blues for several years and watched so many excellent players in the Town shirt. It's hard to pick people out ahead of others but of the great 1981 side that won the UEFA Cup I always liked Frans Thijssen, the Dutch midfielder who looked as if the ball had been stuck to his right boot. Three years on and several members of that team – Paul Cooper, George Burley, Steve McCall, Russell Osman, Terry Butcher, John Wark, Paul

Mariner, Eric Gates and Kevin O'Callaghan – were still going strong. To find myself changing alongside them in the dressing room was both weird and wonderful at the same time. I used to stand in the North Stand and cheer their every move, so the fact that these guys were now chatting to me and putting me at ease was very strange, to say the least.

Big Butch was great with me, I remember. He was quite vociferous in the dressing room beforehand and I was just sitting quietly in the corner, minding my own business. He came across a couple of times and said a few words. A few years later he was still looking after me. He was an established member of the England squad by then and there were a few trips where the seniors and the Under-21 players travelled together. Butch would come and get me to join him for a game of cards with the captain, Bryan Robson, and some other big-name players. It was as if he wanted to make sure I was okay. Not many people can say Terry Butcher was their minder, but I can!

GOING BACK TO THE game against Coventry, I don't honestly recall if Bobby Ferguson had any specific words for me as we trooped out before the kick-off. I was thinking I probably wouldn't get on, and if I did it would be pretty late in the game, but when Eric Gates was injured inside the first 30 minutes and couldn't continue I was told to get ready. There wasn't time to get nervous and as he sent me on Fergie just told me to play my normal game and enjoy myself. We were already 2-0 ahead by then but Paul Mariner was also injured. He had little choice, however, but to stay on and complete what turned out to be his last game for the club – he moved to Arsenal a few days later – as a bit of a passenger out on the right. That meant I was playing virtually on my own up front and when Terry Gibson scored for Coventry to make it 2-1 we just wanted to hear the final whistle to ensure we earned the three points.

I was happy enough with my own performance and thinking how well it had gone, when I was suddenly presented with a chance to mark the occasion in the best way possible, with a goal. We were awarded a free-kick near the half-way line and Terry Butcher pumped the ball into the box. John Wark climbed to get his head to it and knocked it on and I knew immediately that I could get to it first. I was about 10 yards out and I stretched and slid in to make contact on the volley just before Ian Butterworth put in a challenge. The ball looped over the keeper and dropped just under the bar, at which point I was off to celebrate. I even managed to spot a couple of school friends, several of whom were positioned behind the home dug-out, as the rest of the team congratulated me.

My mother, Frances, and my younger sister, Charletta, were also at the game, along with my girlfriend, Leonie, who later became my wife. They were just as excited as I was when the ball went into the net and there wasn't a great deal of time before the referee blew for full-time. A few of my school pals found their way on to the pitch to congratulate me and I was still in a bit of a daze back in the dressing room. It was all a bit crazy and some of the press guys wanted to interview me. But Bobby Ferguson decided I should keep a low profile and asked Russell Osman to make sure I got home safely. Russell had a Mercedes four-wheel drive and I remember being thrilled to get a lift in it. I tried to stay out of sight because I didn't know how to cope with fans looking for autographs and to be honest it was a relief to get home and shut the door behind me.

There was no question of me going out on the town to celebrate because I wasn't old enough. In fact, back then there was only one night club, the First Floor Club, and I became so well known because of the goal that there was no chance of me ever getting in there until I'd turned 18. Had I not scored and had such a high-profile introduction to the first team, I reckon I could have got in there without anyone batting an eyelid. From what I recall, a couple of friends called round to see me and we ended up popping round to one of their houses for a game of pool before I went back to my own place and turned in for the night.

I awoke on the Sunday morning to find several reporters and photographers on my doorstep. The manager had given me strict instructions not to do any interviews or have my picture taken so my mum went to the door to explain the situation. But we did allow Dave Allard to come in because we knew him so well. He worked for the local paper and I had not only come across him several times but had got to know him quite well. Dave had all the Sunday papers with him and I couldn't get my head round the fact that I was featured so prominently in every one of them. He asked a few questions, made a few notes and his photographer colleague fired off a few pictures, so they had a nice 'exclusive' to themselves for Monday's paper.

Later on the Sunday morning I innocently set off with the intention of playing for my youth side, Langham Lions. I didn't want to let my manager, Roy Knightsbridge, down. But it was decided that it might not be a good idea to play and instead I watched from the touchline. I had my boots under my arm and some of the photographers, who had missed me at home and decided to follow me to the ground, were quick to snap me. I still have no idea whether there was anything to stop me playing for Langham, where Stuart Slater, who later played for West Ham, Celtic and then Ipswich, was one of my team-mates. I was only signed by Ipswich as a schoolboy and after the game against Coventry I was handed an envelope that contained £30. It was to cover expenses, I was told, and I was thrilled to bits with what seemed like a lot of money, to me at least, at the time.

ACTUALLY, MY STORY NEARLY never happened at all. At one point there seemed no way that I would be playing for Ipswich. There's a straightforward explanation – they had not shown any interest. There were three other clubs who all wanted me to join them and the first one I visited was Nottingham Forest. I was only about 11 or 12 at the time. They were the European champions and I remember meeting their manager, Brian Clough, who asked me if I was enjoying my time with them. I also went to West Ham, where John Lyall was in charge, and he was really keen that I should sign for the Hammers. I remember playing in a game there and Paul Ince was alongside me in midfield. But I was actually keener to join Luton, a far more successful club back then than they are now. They were in the top division, for a start, and in David Pleat they had a manager who really made me feel wanted.

Ipswich had not even made contact around the time I had made my mind up to join Luton, but they suddenly came on the scene and from that moment on there was only ever going to be one winner. I wasn't disappointed, just surprised, that Town hadn't shown an interest in me but the chief scout, Ron Gray, told me he had been well aware of me for some time and wouldn't have let me slip through the net. Ron didn't see me score on my debut because he was scouting in London but the first thing he did when he came into the club on the Monday morning was to sit down and watch a video recording of my big moment. Ron was a great character and I remember him paying me a tremendous compliment in a newspaper article when he said: "Jason is like Jimmy White in snooker – he's three moves ahead of the opposition."

Having signed schoolboy forms for Town, I was attending a weekly training session every Thursday evening in the Portman Road gymnasium. The man in charge was top defender Allan Hunter, who was coming towards the end of his playing career. He was an excellent teacher and it was just a case of trying to progress and do my very best to ensure I would be taken on full-time once I left school. I went to Lilleshall for the England schoolboy trials but didn't get in, so had anyone suggested that I would play and score at first team level while still attending school, I'd have thought they were completely mad. After my debut I made a further four substitute appearances through to the end of the season and it wasn't until just before Christmas that year, less than a fortnight after my 17th birthday, that I started a game for the first time. It was at Manchester United, of all places, and I played up front alongside Eric Gates as we lost 3-0.

Bobby Ferguson was the first of several managers for whom I played and I can't speak too highly of what he did for me. He was the father I didn't have at home, if you like, and he made me feel a bit special. He never forgot my birthday and at times I felt I could not do anything wrong in Fergie's eyes. I was a bit like the teacher's pet, I suppose. The other lads would give me a bit of stick, but I was never embarrassed about it and the most disappointed I felt for Fergie, apart from when I heard he had been sacked, was when we just failed to win through to the Milk Cup Final in 1985. We played Norwich in the semi-final and being a local boy I loved the derby games. It might even have been the biggest of them all, since there was a Wembley place on offer for the winners.

We dominated the home leg but all we had to show for our superiority was a single goal from Mich D'Avray. However, we firmly believed we were a better team than them, so to go to Carrow Road with a one-goal lead wasn't a bad position to be in. On the night, though, we were beaten 2-0 and their second goal arrived just three minutes from the end when Steve Bruce came flying in to head just under the bar. He was my man but I was blocked off by another of their players and couldn't stop him. It amazed me that a 17 year-old kid was marking their best header of a ball and to this day I wonder how that came about. Norwich virtually kicked us off the park, much to the anger of Fergie. Mich nearly swallowed his tongue after a clash with Dave Watson and Terry Butcher's frustration spilled over when he put his boot through the dressing room door. We all felt Norwich had over-stepped the mark physically and that the ref had done too little to protect us, and when the Canaries were relegated after they won the Milk Cup we all had a chuckle to ourselves.

We were relegated in 1986 and Fergie went the following year, after we finished fifth in the Second Division and were beaten in the play-offs. Only top scorer Kevin Wilson, whose goals earned him a move to Chelsea, and I were ever-present that season. The new manager, John Duncan, was a nice guy and I think he liked me. We went a bit more direct under him and my role changed as I operated just behind the front two of Mich and David Lowe. We had our next change of manager in 1990 when John Lyall took over and I'll never forget his words when we met up – "got you at last" he said with a huge grin on his face. I loved my time with him, as all the players did. His door was always open and if you went to his office intending to have a quick chat it wasn't unusual to still be there a couple of hours later, talking football.

WE WEREN'T FANCIED AT all before the 1991/92 season kicked off. The bookmakers had us down as 25-1 shots and even our own supporters didn't seem to rate our chances because for the first few home games we were playing in front of 8,000–9,000 crowds at Portman Road. The figure gradually improved until the place was packed on the last day of the season after we had made sure of the title the previous week at Oxford, when Gavin Johnson's ninth minute goal earned us a point on a day when a certain Jim Magilton opened the scoring for the home side just two minutes earlier.

We were in at the start of the Premier League and, incredibly, we lost just twice in our opening games. One of the most memorable was our 2-0 win at Norwich just before Christmas. It was live on Sky and when Neil Thompson netted our second goal near the end my brother ran on to the pitch and planted a blue and white Santa-style hat on my head. I still had it on as the game restarted and I could see him being frogmarched out of the stadium by the police.

I had just one season in the new Premiership with Ipswich before I left to join Tottenham. My contract was up in the summer of 1993 and I must have been talking about a new deal, on and off, for about six months. But we couldn't agree on anything and it was stalemate as Celtic and Arsenal both showed interest before Spurs made a firm move. The £1.9 million fee was decided by a tribunal and I remember signing on manager Ossie Ardiles' birthday because he announced at the press conference that he had been out to buy himself a present.

I said some things about having a soft spot for Spurs, which was true, but in the papers it read as if I was trying to say I had been a Tottenham fan all my life. Even now, I get Ipswich fans who say they took great exception to my remarks, but I have to explain that my comments were greatly exaggerated. After Ipswich, I have always liked Tottenham – that's what I actually said, but it came out totally wrong in the papers and I got such a hard time whenever I was out and about in Ipswich. The one mistake I made during my four years at White Hart Lane was to continue to live in Ipswich and make the journey to the training ground on a daily basis. The club didn't like it and moaned about it all the time. I was late for training a few times and it didn't do me any favours. With the benefit of hindsight, I should have definitely moved house and, had I done so, I am convinced I would have done better for Spurs.

Having said that, a lot of my problems were entirely self-inflicted and I wouldn't even attempt to deny it. There is no excuse, for example, for being convicted of drink-driving; sheer stupidity, I would call it. Also, I should have walked away when there was conflict on the horizon. On one occasion, I was out in Ipswich with my pal and former Town team-mate, Chris Kiwomya, who I hadn't seen for a while. We were sitting at the bar of a town centre pub when a guy had a go at us for no apparent reason. I did my best to ignore him but eventually my patience snapped. I'm not a violent person so I picked up the nearest thing to me, which happened to be a pavlova, and stuck it straight in his face. The police were called and they advised both Chris and I to make ourselves scarce, although the story still made the papers.

In my first year at Tottenham the fans were calling me the new Glenn Hoddle. I was even playing well enough to be mentioned in connection with an England call-up, although I failed to progress after being capped at B level. After Ossie was sacked I played for Gerry Francis but although our relationship was fine I faded from the first team picture towards the end of my time at White Hart Lane and I was out of contract when I left in 1997. It was like a dream come true when George Burley, the Ipswich manager, asked me back on a week-to-week basis and I did well enough for him to start discussing a full-time contract. At the time I couldn't have asked for more and I was excited at the thought of coming back.

Things seemed to be going according to plan in my second spell at Portman Road. I played nine games and scored twice but the Coca-Cola Cup fourth round success at Oxford, when I put us on the way to a 2-1 win, proved to be my last outing for the club. When I went in for training at Bent Lane a couple of days later I was told I would be with Dale Roberts' group and I didn't think anything of it. Then my name was absent from the squad for the Saturday league game at Reading and I knew something was up. I went to see George, who said my time was up and I better look for another club. I wasn't suicidal but it took me a very long time to get over it; in fact to this day I don't think I have ever properly recovered from the shock of being told I was finished at Ipswich.

I cannot say for sure what convinced George to dispense with my services, but from what I could gather he had received information that I had been out drinking a couple of weeks earlier. Not only that, but he had also been informed that I had been bad-mouthing him. I swear it wasn't true. I played in a 1-1 midweek draw at Birmingham but had to come off because I wasn't feeling well and even though I wasn't able to train over the next few days I declared myself fit for the game at Charlton the following Saturday. It was wrong of me to say I was okay to play and I accept that, but I was so keen to make an impression and earn a contract that I even convinced myself I had recovered fully from a virus, although that was far from the case. We lost the game 3-0 and I was laid low when we were beaten at home by Stockport the following Tuesday.

I was back in the team as we drew at home with Sheffield United and then away at Wolves before the Coca-Cola Cup win at Oxford, and as far as I was concerned all was well. What I didn't know, however, was that George had received information that I not only broke a curfew in the week of the Charlton game but that I had also said some uncomplimentary things about him. I did my best to plead my case and it hurt that he was prepared to go on hearsay. He said he didn't think he could trust me and that was that – I was finished with Ipswich just when it seemed I was on the brink of a fresh start there, something I'd set my heart on doing.

I was grateful when Ian Atkins took me to Northampton and I scored six goals in 25 games to help them reach the League One play-offs, but their style of play didn't really suit me and I moved on to Colchester, where I played more than 100 games before an arthritic toe problem made it impossible for me to continue and I had no alternative but to retire in 2002. After that I managed Ridgeons League teams Ipswich Wanderers and Leiston, both with some success.

At my peak with Tottenham I was earning very good money, but nothing in comparison to what today's Premiership stars are picking up. However, I don't have to be told I should have more to show for my time in the game, although there are plenty of ex-players who could say the same.

On a personal note, I am divorced from Leonie but we remain friends and she is a wonderful mother to my three sons – Dion, who was born in my time at Tottenham and whose godfather is Sol Campbell, Andre and Emille. I have a great relationship with them. Andre is with the Town academy so there might even be another Dozzell in the first team in a few years.

I grew up not knowing my own father, who went back to the States when I was two. It wasn't easy being a black American serviceman in Ipswich 40 years ago but the good news is that I was reunited with him when I was about 19 and we now get on really well. I try to make it out there to see him once a year. Overall, I still think there are a lot of positives in my story and that I didn't do too badly in a career that saw me play over 600 games and score more than 100 goals.

JIM MAGILTON
MIDFIELDER 1999-2006

BORN 6 May 1969, Belfast

SIGNED 22 March 1999 from Sheffield Wednesday, £682,500, following loan spell

IPSWICH CAREER 315 games, 21 goals

HONOURS First Division Play-Off Final 1999-2000, 52 Northern Ireland caps

LEFT Played his last game for the club in May 2006, appointed manager the following month

His initial stay at Portman Road might only have been a few months, having been signed on loan from Sheffield Wednesday, but his first few appearances were enough to convince then manager George Burley that the Northern Ireland international should be signed permanently. Magilton had been frozen out at Hillsborough and was grateful for the chance to get his career back on track and he quickly became a firm favourite with supporters who appreciated his ability to make the team tick with his range of passing skills and ability to open up opposition defences. It seemed he would be on his way when his contract expired in 2006 but after an emotional farewell that extended to a well deserved lap of honour he instead launched a successful bid to become Joe Royle's successor and half-way through his second season in charge he was rewarded with a new contract to keep him at the club until 2010.

Ipswich Town 5 v Bolton Wanderers 3 (after extra-time)

First Division Play-off semi-final, second leg
Wednesday 17 May 2000

Portman Road
Attendance 21,543

*After failing at the same hurdle in each of the previous three seasons,
Ipswich win a titanic clash and Jim Magilton scores the only senior
hat-trick of his 674-game playing career*

Teams

George Burley	**Managers**	Sam Allardyce
Richard Wright		Jussi Jaaskelainen
Wayne Brown		Gudni Bergsson
(Sub. Martijn Reuser)		
Tony Mowbray		Mark Fish
Mark Venus		Mike Whitlow
Gary Croft		Paul Warhurst
		(Sub. Franck Passi)
Matt Holland		Paul Ritchie
Jim Magilton		Claus Jensen
James Scowcroft		Michael Johansen
(Sub. Richard Naylor)		(Sub. Jimmy Phillips)
Jamie Clapham		Robbie Elliott
David Johnson		Dean Holdwsorth
		(Sub. Bo Hansen)
Marcus Stewart		Allan Johnston
Magilton 18 pen, 49, 90, Clapham 94 pen, Reuser 109	Goals	Holdsworth 6, 39, Johnston 50

Referee: Barry Knight (Orpington)

BE HONEST – YOU DIDN'T think I was going to pick any other game bar this one, did you? It was an absolute banker, by far the most amazing match of my life, and I could not have chosen any other.

To fully transmit the unbelievable drama and tension of the second game against Bolton at Portman Road, it is important to mention what happened in the first game at the Reebok Stadium because if I'm totally honest I was fearing the very worst after we were all over the place for the first 25 minutes or so and trailed 2-0.

The previous year we had gone out in the play-offs to Bolton and I wasn't the only player thinking 'Please, no, not again' as we not only conceded two goals but also lost our organiser-in-chief, Tony Mowbray, the guy who knitted all the bits and pieces together and kept everybody focused on their jobs, to injury.

Okay, we had a few leaders in that side – Matt Holland, the skipper, was obviously one, John McGreal, Mark Venus, Marcus Stewart, yours truly – but Mogga was the main man and we all knew it. He was also the first team coach by then and so had a tremendous influence on the team and how we played.

I remember how Eidur Gudjohnsen, Bolton's Icelandic international, was in terrific form up there – so was Dean Holdsworth – and they both scored goals. I couldn't really work out how a team with so many good players were even in the play-offs. I was actually thinking to myself 'How is it that Bolton have not won automatic promotion and how come we're not going up with them?'

The answer, of course, was that Charlton Athletic, who had been outstanding and had stayed out in front all season, won the title and Manchester City and ourselves were locked in a battle for the second automatic promotion place that went to the very last day of the regular league programme before it was resolved in their favour, leaving Ipswich to negotiate the play-offs for the fourth year in a row. To be frank, I will always think we blew it as far as finishing in the top two was concerned.

At 2-0 down at the Reebok Stadium, and remembering how miserable it had been to lose to Bolton the previous year, I was thinking 'I can't believe this is going to happen to us all over again – and to the same team'. After 10 months of hard slog and giving it everything we had, I couldn't bear to think that we were going to go out with barely a whimper.

It seemed things were going from bad to worse. As if being two goals behind and losing Mogga wasn't bad enough, we then saw David Johnson go off with a neck problem after he collided with Mark Fish. But within the space of about three minutes Marcus Stewart scored a real wonder goal from about 30 yards that gave us a lifeline and come the interval we went in questioning whether Bolton could come back out and play so well again – in other words, could they repeat what had been a very good first-half display?

Wayne Brown had replaced Mogga and Martijn Reuser was on for Johnno, and we went out for the second half thinking we could at least level the scores. In what seemed no time at all I remember I missed a great chance, scraping the crossbar with a first-time shot after the ball dropped to me on the edge of the box, or we might have actually won it 3-2.

As it was, though, we were quite happy to settle for 2-2 as a result of Marcus' second goal and because we were also aware that Claus Jensen had missed a great chance for Bolton or they might have pipped us on the day. So it was very much a case of all square and everything to play for ahead of the second game and from feeling very low when we were 2-0 down, the fact that we had pulled level definitely perked us all up and made us believe we could complete the job back at our own place.

The tie was finely balanced and there was no doubt that both teams badly wanted to win it. Ipswich had been beaten semi-finalists in each of the previous three years, while Bolton had beaten us in 1999 but lost out to Watford in the final. The prospect of spending another season in what was then called the First Division was no doubt dreaded by both of us.

There is no doubt that we had gained a massive lift from the fact that we had managed to recover well and draw the first game 2-2. Not only did we fight back from falling 2-0 behind pretty early on, we felt it was Bolton who were hanging on towards the end of the match and there was no lack of confidence in our camp, while the mood around the town told us the supporters were also in a positive frame of mind about the outcome.

Despite its obvious importance, we prepared as we would have done for any other midweek game and for my own part I went off at lunchtime to fill up on pasta at a town centre restaurant that was a regular haunt of some of us. I had Gary Croft and Jermaine Wright with me and I remember our assistant manager, Dale Roberts, was also there because I recall him shouting over more than once to our waiter and telling him "Make sure that lot don't have any chips". The banter was great and the atmosphere relaxed, with each and every one of us eagerly looking ahead to that night's game.

Another part of my normal midweek home match routine was to have a few hours, usually about three, in bed in the afternoon. It was rare that I slept the whole time because I tended to replay my own last game – and every other player's – in my head. On this occasion I expected to replay every kick of the first game against Bolton and to think about the second one but as soon as my head hit the pillow I was off.

I slept so well it was scary. Three solid hours, which had never happened to me before, and nor did it happen again right through to my very last game six years later. The feeling I experienced that day was a complete one-off. I couldn't believe it because I would normally stick a DVD on to help me relax but on this occasion I drifted straight off to sleep and the next thing I knew I was waking up feeling unbelievably relaxed and ready for the game.

I remember jumping in the car and driving the short distance into town and to the ground, and I couldn't believe how good I felt. I saw lots of fans and I gave them the thumbs-up as they waved and shouted, and I recall thinking to myself how amazingly relaxed I felt. Normally you have the butterflies twitching in your stomach, which tends to give you a bit of an edge, but there was none of that. It was like I was floating on air, so calm, and I just knew it was going to be a very special night.

EVEN NOW, THE HAIRS on the back of my neck are standing to attention as I remember that whole night. I was convinced it was going to be like nothing I'd ever experienced before and I knew for sure that I was not going to be disappointed the way I had been the previous year, just as I knew for sure this was going to be Ipswich's night and that we would all be going to Wembley for the play-off final.

Anyone reading this will probably wonder how I could have been so confident and I wouldn't want you to confuse that with complacency. Within myself I knew – as far as it is possible to know – that it would be our turn to celebrate, but I also knew we were in for a real ding-dong game because both sides had so many good players and, in particular, good attacking players.

It was us or them, a fight to the death – that was my thinking as I walked into the dressing room and when I saw George Burley, the gaffer, I became even more determined. At that precise moment I had a picture in my head of George one year earlier, following our defeat by Bolton, and I could see him looking utterly devastated that a third successive play-off attempt had failed.

I owed George a lot because he brought me to Ipswich on loan when I was at a very low point in my career and when he decided he wanted to sign me on a permanent basis it gave me an enormous lift. Form training with the kids at Sheffield Wednesday I was made to feel important again by turning out regularly for an ambitious club with an eye on the Premiership. There and then, I remember telling myself 'This is the night when you repay George for the faith he showed in you'.

There was a calmness about the place that fitted in with the way I was feeling. I was surrounded by players who knew what it was like to lose a play-off game – Richard Wright, Fabian Wilnis, Jamie Clapham, Tony Mowbray, Mark Venus, Matt Holland, David Johnson and James Scowcroft had all been alongside me the previous year. In the case of Wrighty and Scowie, still youngsters in football terms, they had suffered in each of the previous three years, and I was determined that this time there would be no heartbreak, that we were going all the way.

Regardless of what the 90 minutes – or two hours as it turned out to be – held in store Ipswich were going to Wembley and absolutely nothing was going to stop us. It was obvious, after I got changed and went out on the pitch, that there was a special atmosphere inside Portman Road, different to other occasions, and three things happened that gave us a massive lift ahead of the kick-off.

Firstly, Mogga passed fit. Secondly, so did Johnno. We would have both our casualties from the first game. Thirdly, Eidur Gudjohnsen failed a fitness test. When I heard Gudjohnsen was out I felt even more optimistic about our chances. He was their best player, something of a talisman, and without his threat in attack there was no question in my mind that Bolton would be far less effective. I know George felt exactly the same and it's quite normal in football to get a lift when you see the opposition line-up and realise that they have been weakened by the absence of their star player.

George always tended to concentrate on his own side when he gave his team talk prior to us going out and that's something I picked up from him that I try to do myself as a manager. He had one or two points to make about Bolton, things he said we should look out for, but basically he just drummed it into us that it was up to us to perform.

As soon as we got started I knew I was going to have a good game. I could see every picture – by that I mean that even before the ball was passed to me I knew exactly what was and wasn't on. I felt unbelievably good. We had an early chance when Paul Ritchie sent the ball straight to the feet of Johnno, who ran through and forced a full-length save from Jussi Jaaskelainen. Then Wayne Brown, who was preferred to Manuel Thetis in the starting line-up, made a mistake when he was caught in possession by Michael Johansen, who spotted Wrighty off his line and from near enough the half-way line he sent the ball over Wrighty's head and on to the roof of the net.

At that moment I was thinking 'Oh my God, here we go' and it was even worse when Bolton went ahead. It was only six minutes in but it seemed ages since the kick-off. From Johansen's up and under Robbie Elliott went up to challenge Wrighty, who didn't get hold of the ball and it dropped for Holdsworth to poke it over the line. Wrighty complained he had been fouled but I wasn't so sure. So we were 1-0 down, which clearly gave them a massive lift, but it seemed to lift us as well and we set off in search of the equaliser.

Johnno, who had seen an earlier shot saved by Jaaskelainen, connected with a low cross from the left but flicked it wide using the outside of his right foot. Then came the moment when I pulled us level.

Crofty took a throw-in and I swapped passes with him before I fed the ball into Johnno and got it back again. By this time I'm making my way into the penalty area and I could see Holdsworth coming over. I'm thinking 'What's he doing here?' because you don't often see a centre-forward in a defensive position. I just knew he was going to stick a leg out, which he did by bringing his right leg round behind him, and as I nutmegged him he brought me down. It was a clear penalty. It seemed everything had slowed down right at that moment and I went over his trailing right leg.

The referee gave the penalty straight away but the Bolton players were seething. Mike Whitlow stuck a finger in my face and was screaming "You're a cheat". Paul Ritchie gave me a shove and I sort of squared up to him and he stuck his head into mine. It was all going off and the rest of their players were milling around far from happy.

There was no point in me getting involved. We had been awarded a penalty, rightly so in my opinion, and I wanted to stay nice and calm. Once the hullabaloo died down I knew I was going to score and although their keeper went the right way, low to his right, he was nowhere near getting it. As I turned back to celebrate there was Whitlow in my face again having a moan but I just got back to the centre circle to get re-started.

At that moment the stadium seemed to erupt and it never really calmed down again. That loud buzz was there for the rest of the game and the atmosphere was so electric. The only way I can describe what it was like is to say that it seemed the supporters were reaching out, picking players up and giving them a shake. The penalty made it 1-1 and it was game on again as far as we were concerned.

We were getting close to half-time when Crofty gave away a free-kick as he challenged Allan Johnston and we had to organise ourselves to defend it. Bolton had several players round the ball and three of them dummied it before Holdsworth hit it. We had seven players in the wall but he still managed to steer his low shot round the wall and in off the far post. Wrighty saw it late and by the time he dived the ball was virtually in the net.

So we were trailing again but there was still time for another large slice of drama before the interval. Veno pushed the ball through, I dummied it and it ran on for Stewie in the box. He was tackled by Ritchie and although there was slight contact with the ball he also took Stewie's legs away. As the referee blew and pointed to the spot he was immediately crowded out by the Bolton lads and he was backing away so much that he ended up close to the corner flag. He flashed the yellow card a few times before things calmed down but after I had spotted the ball and was waiting to take the kick Whitlow walked past and stood on my foot.

I flicked my leg out and at that point Paul Warhurst got involved, being very vociferous. The ref called the pair of us together and I just muttered something about it being a big occasion with a lot of stake. They were doing their utmost to put me off but I wasn't going to allow myself to be wound up. In the end, though, I beat myself.

What is the cardinal sin of penalty taking? That's right, changing your mind at the last moment. I knew Jaaskelainen would dive the same way as he had done for the first one and I just kept repeating to myself 'Put it in the other corner, put it in the other corner' over and over again. As I placed the ball on the spot, as I walked back, even as I ran forward and was about to make contact with the ball, I swear I still intended sticking it to the keeper's left but for some unknown reason I changed my mind. Honest to God, I was so clear in my thinking until the very last second and it was as if an outside force was at work.

I WENT IN AT half-time thinking I had let myself down, but more importantly the team. Dale Roberts was very supportive and said "Don't worry about it, you still have another 45 minutes to get the right result" but

Mogga, ever the realist, told me in no uncertain terms "If we get another penalty you're not hitting it". I said something like "Just let me get over this miss first, will you?" George's team talk was a blur to me. I just kept thinking about the penalty miss and couldn't get it out of my head.

Before going back out I went through to the toilets and slipped into one of the cubicles. I closed the door behind me and said a little prayer. "Please, God, whatever else you can do to me, don't let that penalty miss cost us," I said, then I threw a bit of cold water over my face and I was ready to go out for the second half.

We had only been going about four minutes when I scored to make it 2-2. Veno played a great ball into Johnno, who nicked it in front of Whitlow and put me clear. I dropped my shoulder as I went forward into the box. There was another nutmeg on Warhurst, then I went past Johnston and I was thinking 'Bloody hell, what am I doing in here?' as I kept going and fired into the top corner at the near post to level it at 2-2.

The noise at that point was incredible but I didn't really have time to enjoy it because Bolton went ahead yet again just a minute later. Holdsworth chested down a long pass from the back and Johnston hit a real wonder goal, a fabulous 25-yard shot that flew over Wrighty. For a split second I said to myself 'It's not going to be our night' but as soon as we kicked off again the doom and gloom had lifted and I was thinking 'Yes, we can still win this'.

Johnno had a great chance virtually straight from the kick-off, only to be denied by a great save from Jaaskelainen, and then we had to make a change when Scowie felt his hamstring and was replaced by Richard Naylor. There was no let-up as far as the action was concerned and Wrighty made a great save with his left leg to prevent Claus Jensen making it 4-2 when he was through one on one. A goal then and it would have been curtains but instead we managed to claw our way level for a third time inside the last minute. Veno was virtually on the half-way line when he pumped the ball forward to Mogga, who was under pressure from Mark Fish. The way Mogga arched his back, and his body shape, told me he was going to get a head on it and I read the situation perfectly. 'This is going to land at my feet' I was telling myself and as it did I could see what I had to do – hit it with the outside of my right foot through the legs of Ritchie, who was between me and the goal. That's exactly what I did, although the other lads all claimed I'd scuffed it and the goal was a bit of a fluke.

As soon as I hit the ball I knew it was on its way and I actually started to celebrate before it had even crossed the line. It was pandemonium and I ended up flat on my back with the rest of the lads piling on top of me. There was a supporter, too, giving me a hug and I shrugged him off as I got to my feet. We heard there was to be four minutes of stoppage time and, would you believe, I had a chance to win it for us. Whitlow brought down Stewie and was sent off, and from the free-kick I hit the ball well over. But when the referee blew for the end of the 90 minutes I knew we would go on to win because I could tell by looking at the Bolton players that they had 'gone' by then.

INTO EXTRA-TIME AND THEY were down to ten men when Ritchie manhandled Johnno and wrestled him to the ground inside the area. Incredibly, we had a third penalty and as I walked up Mogga had to restrain me. In one ear I had Veno shouting "Go on, hit it" but Mogga was also telling me "You can't take it". The three of us were having a real squabble when Jamie Clapham piped up "We've got to get on with it – I'll hit it". I relented and I was thinking that Mogga didn't trust me, although I also realised he was just worried that the keeper had the Indian sign on me. He was proved right when Jamie banged the ball straight down the middle to score and put us 4-3 ahead.

Bolton were probably thinking the gods were conspiring against them but the way they lost their discipline hardly helped. When Elliott clattered substitute Martijn Reuser he was sent off for a second yellow card and could hardly have any complaints. They also had Holdsworth struggling so they were virtually down to eight men. Crofty also came close to scoring when he hit a shot on to the roof of the net towards the end of the first half of extra time. There were fans dancing on top of the executive boxes – the party was well under way – when Bam-Bam (Richard Naylor) held off Ritchie and sent 'Rolls' Reuser away to score our fifth goal with a left-foot shot that flew across Jaaskelainen into the far top corner. As the ball hit the net I was thinking 'I'm going to play at Wembley – and I'm going there to win'.

Wrighty made a great save to prevent Ritchie heading a fourth goal for Bolton and when the whistle finally went I was in the far corner of the ground. With hundreds of fans running towards me I decided to sprint to the dressing room. I was thinking 'Just get me to Wembley' because I'd been there as a spectator and I'd sat on the bench for Liverpool when we played Manchester United in the Charity Shield. But I hadn't played at Wembley and that was one ambition, barring injury, which I was looking forward to realising.

I ended up sitting in the home dressing room on my own for ages as the rest of the players were being mobbed out on the pitch. It seemed like a very long time before they eventually trooped in. I got plenty of stick along the lines "Who said you couldn't run?" The atmosphere was electric and the room was rocking so much I could feel the vibrations. The gaffer said to us all "Fantastic, well done, enjoy your night – but don't forget we've a game still to play". It was music to my ears.

Full marks to the Bolton lads because we all knew how they felt. That had been us the previous year so we knew what they were going through. To a man they all came up to me before they left Portman Road that night and congratulated me. They were saying "Well done, now go on and win it" and I couldn't speak highly enough of them. Even Holdsworth, who was in the treatment room having stitches, made a point of congratulating us all.

THAT NIGHT WE WENT INTO town and I'd never seen Ipswich like that before. There was such a strong feeling of goodwill among everyone we bumped into. We were all delighted to have overcome that hurdle of getting to Wembley, that we hadn't wasted a whole season's hard work. We still had about 12 days to go before the final but every single player was firmly focused on it. There might have been a few sore heads the next morning but there was no danger of complacency setting in.

In all the commotion I never even got the match ball for scoring my hat-trick. Would you believe that someone nicked it? Instead I got one of the spares signed by all the lads and even when someone, whose conscience presumably got the better of him, produced the actual match ball some time later I wasn't bothered. I let him keep it. My father has the autographed ball over in Belfast and when I go back home it's like Lord of the Rings when he says "Do you want to see the ball?" I have told him – and I meant it – that if we had gone to Wembley and lost I'd have put a knife through it. Yes, it was the match of my life, but without us going on to beat Barnsley it wouldn't have meant even half as much to me.

TONY MOWBRAY
CENTRE-HALF 1995-2001

BORN 22 November 1963, Saltburn
SIGNED 6 October 1995 from Celtic, £300,000
IPSWICH CAREER 152 games, 8 goals
HONOURS Promotion to Premiership 1999-2000
LEFT Became first team coach, appointed manager of Hibernian in May 2004

Tony was an inspirational captain of Ipswich, just as he was of previous clubs Middlesbrough and Celtic, and it was at Portman Road that he took his first steps towards becoming a manager when George Burley appointed him as first team coach in 1999. His playing days were far from over, however, and he returned to the side as Town finally realised their promotion dream with a play-off final win at Wembley that was to bring down the curtain on his playing career. After a spell of more than two years in charge of Scottish side Hibernian, he was appointed manager of West Bromwich Albion in October 2006 and after being beaten in the play-off final the following year he led them to the Championship title in 2008.

Ipswich Town 4 v Barnsley 2

First Division Play-off final
Monday 29 May 2000

Wembley Stadium
Attendance 73,427

After several near misses since being relegated five years earlier, Ipswich finally negotiate the play-offs to book a return ticket to the Premiership

Teams

George Burley	**Managers**	Dave Bassett
Richard Wright		Kevin Miller
John McGreal		John Curtis
		(Sub. Nicky Eaden)
Tony Mowbray		Darren Barnard
Mark Venus		Chris Morgan
Gary Croft		Steve Chettle
Matt Holland		Keith Brown
Jim Magilton		Matty Appleby
Jermaine Wright		Craig Hignett
(Sub. Fabian Wilnis)		
Jamie Clapham		Neil Shipperley
David Johnson		Bruce Dyer
(Sub. Richard Naylor)		(Sub. Georgi Hristov)
Marcus Stewart		Eric Tinkler
(Sub. Martijn Reuser)		(Sub. Geoff THomas)
Mowbray 28, Naylor 52, Stewart 58, Reuser 90	Goals	R Wright 6 (own goal), Hignett 78 (pen)

Referee: Terry Heilbron (Newton Aycliffe)

EVERY SINGLE PROFESSIONAL FOOTBALLER, never mind the thousands, or maybe even millions, of kids wanting to follow in their footsteps, probably dreams of playing at Wembley at some point in his career. But only a small minority are lucky enough to achieve their ambition and, of those, only a tiny number also manage to mark the occasion by scoring a goal. I was lucky on both counts so I could hardly choose any other game than the one that proved to be my very last as a player, although at the time I promise you I had absolutely no idea that would prove to be the case.

It was then, and still is today, the richest football match in the world. Back in 2000, if my memory serves me correctly, it was dubbed the £10 million game in reference to the money the winning club could expect to bank from being members of the Premiership the following season. I think the prize fund, taking into consideration the parachute payments that come into effect in the event of relegation, has increased about seven fold since then and I found out what it is like to be on the losing side in 2006 when my West Bromwich Albion side was narrowly beaten by Derby County. The irony, of course, is that I played in the last play-off final to be staged at the old Wembley and then led out my team for the first one at the revamped national stadium, a double achievement of which I am extremely proud, even if the outcome on each occasion was not the same.

My abiding memory of the 2000 play-off final is that for the first 15 minutes or so my legs felt as if they were made of jelly. I was a very experienced player but it was almost as if I couldn't budge. I'm glad to say I have never been stuck in quicksand, but I think I know how it might feel. I was not alone because in speaking to the other players I learned they were all feeling pretty much the same and we all agreed that it seemed the emotion in the air was sucking nearly all the energy out of our legs.

We had come through an amazing game against Bolton, the second leg of the semi-final at Portman Road. It is one of those games that will live long in the memories of everyone who witnessed it, as well as those who played in it, what with eight goals, three penalties, moments of controversy and two red cards for our opponents as it ebbed and flowed throughout. Not unfamiliar territory for Ipswich at the time, however, since we had also reached the play-offs in 1997, 1998 and 1999, but this was different, thankfully, in that we progressed beyond the semi-final stage and were destined to take part in the big one. And at Wembley!

The realisation that, at the fourth time of trying, we were finally going to play at Wembley struck a chord with every one of the players and we also realised what it would mean to the fans. For my own part, it was an opportunity I was relishing so late in my playing career. I regarded it as a real blessing because the only other time I had been part of a team going to Wembley was 10 years earlier with Middlesbrough, when we qualified for the Zenith Data Systems Cup Final against Chelsea. Sadly, I missed out through injury, although the manager – Colin Todd had not long taken over from Bruce Rioch – very kindly allowed me to lead out the team, which was an honour in itself and the next best thing to being the skipper. We lost that game 1-0 and I suppose by the time I had been appointed first team coach at Ipswich in 1999 it would be fair to say that I regarded my chances of playing at Wembley as being somewhat limited.

THAT SEASON, 1999/2000, we had started well by winning our first three league games – home victories over Nottingham Forest, who had new manager David Platt in charge for the very first time, and Bolton Wanderers either side of an away success over Swindon – before drawing 2-2 at Sheffield United, a game where I went on as a 66th minute substitute for Mick Stockwell. Ten games into our league programme it was still my only first team football but all that was about to change after we suffered successive defeats, 2-1 at Grimsby and 4-1 at home to Queen's Park Rangers, when Matt Holland gave us a third minute lead and everything seemed to go wrong thereafter, including a red card for Jim Magilton.

I remember how, the previous summer, manager George Burley asked me to pop in and see him, and at first I was a bit concerned. When I saw him he explained that John Gorman, who had joined us the previous year after he had been assistant to Glenn Hoddle with England, had decided to leave and he wanted me to replace him. I was pleasantly surprised and quick to accept because I had never made any secret of the fact that I wanted to go into management and I saw the job as first team coach as an important step towards achieving my ambition.

At that stage I did not expect to be playing first team football again, unless there was some sort of emergency. It was semi-retirement, I suppose, but after the defeat by QPR we were due to take on the league leaders, Charlton, at Portman Road just three days later. George informed me that he had decided to recall me and I remember thinking to myself 'What a game for your comeback'. Anyhow, we managed to defeat Charlton 4-2, which launched us on a tremendous run right through to the end of the season. At one stage we went 18 games without a single defeat and in the final reckoning, from that Charlton game onwards, it was a mere six defeats in 36 games. Charlton were champions with 91 points, Manchester City clinched runners-up spot on the last day to finish with 89 and, despite our own run of form, beating Walsall only took us to within two points of Joe Royle's team.

Having seen off Bolton in that truly remarkable play-off game I mentioned earlier, it would be fair to say that we were confident about the outcome at Wembley. Not over-confident, but I would not deny that we had a hunch it was going to be our year. We had suffered a number of heart-breaking disappointments and we didn't want to be labelled 'nearly men' all over again. You could probably compare it to a situation when a team enjoys a good run in a certain cup competition, starts to believe their name could be on the trophy and invariably goes on to win it. There was also the fact that we had a very good team and over our two league games against Barnsley we had not only won them both, but we had also scored eight times to their once. So, although it had no direct bearing on the outcome at Wembley, it was nevertheless something from which we benefited psychologically as it gave us a slight edge going into the all-important final.

We knew that if we played to our maximum we could win the game, although we certainly did not lose sight of the fact that Barnsley, who had been relegated from the Premiership the previous year, had some decent players. They could hurt us, just as they had hurt Birmingham City at the semi-final stage, establishing a 4-0 lead from the first game at St Andrews. Craig Hignett was someone who was in good form, Neil Shipperley could be a handful and in Bruce Dyer they had a player who, if he was allowed to use the wide open spaces of Wembley to run at our defence, could be a big, big danger. Generally speaking, over the 90 minutes we managed to suffocate those threats and not allow Barnsley too many opportunities, but that is not to say we had an entirely comfortable 90 minutes, without a fright here and there, either.

Before I concentrate on the game itself, I feel it is important to mention that by the time I was recalled to the first team for that win over Charlton I was fairly immobile. I had never been that quick in the first place, to be honest, but in 1999, just a month before my 36th birthday, there was no disguising the fact that pace was quite a way down my list of assets. But right from the very beginning of my playing career, until the very end, I used imagery to assist me. Dream is too strong a word, but I would have pictures in my mind to help psyche myself up. I wanted to be the best header of a ball, someone that no opponent could beat in the air, so the night before a game and even in the dressing room beforehand, when I would sit there and close my eyes, I would see the opposition goalkeeper taking a goal-kick and me getting my timing right to leap above my direct opponent, their centre-forward, and power headers back upfield. On occasions, while I would never see myself scoring the exact goal I headed at Wembley, I would envisage towering above a defender to meet a free-kick or a corner and hanging in the air to head into the net. I would have the feeling of almost flying.

There were no psychologists around in football when I started in the early 80s but from an early age I used imagery. It was something I felt I needed to do. I knew my strengths, my assets, as a player, but I was also very, very aware of my weaknesses. I realised that to make a career out of football I would have to be dominant at something. I would try to hide my deficiencies. I would imagine trying to win races against players I knew were faster than I was and there would be days when I would be so strong and confident that I would find the extra yard in my head. The older you get as a player, the easier it becomes. You see things quicker, so I wasn't too concerned about coming up against a younger, faster opponent. I knew I could be two yards ahead of him when his full-back knocked the ball down the channel and I would be there waiting for it.

Looking back, I have no doubt that my best years as a player were those last few at Ipswich. Not only did I feel I was in control of my own job, but also that I could control the whole team. It was almost as if I was pulling the strings. Like I've said, I was immobile, so I had to have ways of compensating. I made sure I didn't let a hole develop on my right side because the full-back was going upfield all the time. I would get hold of Fabian (Wilnis) or whoever and say "Listen, just sit there and deliver. Don't go pressing their wide man. As soon as you do that their full-back will knock it over your head and I'll have to go out near the corner flag". I didn't want to be out near the corner flag. I wanted to be in the middle, heading the ball out. I would also tell the central midfielders to cut out the passes into the opposition strikers, so the other team would have to look at alternative methods of trying to break us down. It was self-protection, if you like, but I also believe it helped the team to be more solid and the run we had through to the end of the season tends to support that theory.

But back to Wembley. Our preparation was good and there was no lack of belief within the squad. I remember it was a warm day, which must have made it very pleasant for the spectators, but as a player you tend to favour cooler weather, a bit overcast, drizzling even, so the surface has a bit of zip to it. We knew all about the expectancy among our supporters as we had all sorts of people coming up to us in the days beforehand. It was so obvious, as they wished us all the best, that they fully expected us to beat Barnsley and I suppose there was a bit of pressure on us to go out there and make sure the job was done.

Putting it mildly, we did not get off to a very good start when Barnsley took the lead in the sixth minute through a rather freakish own goal. Hignett hit a decent shot and it came back off the crossbar, struck Richard Wright and bounced over the line. At that point you know it's going to be an uphill task. They had done what we'd have liked to have done by getting off to a flier and the next thing I remember is the raw emotion of heading the equaliser to put us back in the game. A corner was cleared and Jim (Magilton) sent in the perfect cross for me to rise and head into the net – yes, just as I had imagined I might.

I have pictures at home of me after I scored and there is a look of unbelievable relief on my face. I recall that after the ball flew into the net I peeled away, looking to run and find my wife, Amber, in the crowd. You want to share moments like that with the people you love and I had a large number of them at the game, including my parents, my sister, her husband and my younger brother, along with some people from my first wife's family, including her father, who had travelled down from Scotland. But I wasn't fast enough to get away and the next thing I knew I was completely swamped by my team-mates. At that point, once things settle down, you know the importance of the next goal and just before half-time Barnsley were awarded a penalty. Hignett was a clever player who put his body between Wrighty and the ball, and as he went to go round the keeper he knew what he was doing in going down under the challenge. But Darren Barnard missed – or rather Wrighty saved it – and in the circumstances we were delighted at going into the dressing room all square at 1-1.

We had been forced into an early change, when Bam-Bam (Richard Naylor) replaced Johnno (David Johnson). We will never know what would have happened had Johnno been able to continue. He was outstanding for Ipswich for a number of years – a threat in every game he played – and he possessed a tremendous scoring record. It was a real shame for him that he had to come off when he did. Bam-Bam, a Yorkshireman, came on and roughed Barnsley up. Take my word for it, just because he's not 6 feet 5 inches tall it doesn't mean he's not a monster. Put it this way – I don't know a stronger player. It's not all about his physique, though, because he also has a determination and desire about him, which can be put down to his upbringing.

Bam-Bam is regarded as a defender these days, but whether he's playing at the back or up front he's not the type you would want to be up against. He gave Barnsley's defenders a really torrid time and the second half hadn't been going very long when he scored our second goal, which was a real breakthrough for us. It was a cool finish, as well, as he controlled the knock-down from Marcus (Stewart) and tucked it away. Bam-Bam was off behind the goal celebrating and pulled his shirt off to show that powerful physique of his. He was booked for unsporting conduct, which I have always felt is a strange way to describe removing your shirt to celebrate a goal.

We were on a high and controlling the game at that point, so you can probably imagine the lift that a third goal just seven minutes later gave us. Marcus got his head to Jamie's (Clapham) cross and steered his header away from the keeper, a top finish from a top player. There still wasn't an hour on the clock but a two-goal cushion was very welcome and I had no doubt that we could see it through, although I have to admit that after Barnsley scored their second goal from a penalty it was probably the longest 11 minutes of my life.

I thought it was a very soft penalty and to be honest I don't particularly like to relive it. I would far rather talk about that headed equaliser. Fatigue, exhaustion, call it what you like, but it played a part in what happened. Geoff Thomas chased a pass that was played over our midfield and down the left, and when he got to it he dragged the ball back inside, at which point I more or less collided with him. My momentum took me into him and I was genuinely shocked when the ref blew for a penalty, which Hignett duly converted. It was something we could have done without, but we had no option but to get on with it.

We were still ahead but that goal certainly lifted Barnsley and they had a real go to pull level and force an extra 30 minutes. I was thinking to myself that if they did manage to equalise I would have had to fear for us in extra time. We'd almost 'gone' as they say. We were pretty much an old defence. John McGreal, for example, wasn't as fit as he would have wanted because he had played so little football towards the end of that season through injury and I know he was dreading the thought of another 15 minutes each way. We were hanging on and we survived a massive scare in the 83rd minute when Barnsley substitute Georgi Hristov was able to get in a header right in front of goal but fortunately Wrighty made an excellent instinctive save to keep the ball out.

There was a mixture of relief and ecstasy to come when Bam-Bam's pass released Martijn (Reuser) to break away and run about 40 yards before firing our fourth goal. We knew that was it and that all the mental torture we had been forced to endure in previous years had finally been worthwhile. When the final whistle sounded we were all hugging and looking up to the stand for our family and friends before we went up the steps to receive the trophy, at which point it was abundantly clear what the result meant to chairman David Sheepshanks and the other Ipswich directors sat nearby in the Royal Box.

THE CELEBRATIONS NEVER really ended. We got back to Ipswich and there was a party at Trinity Park, in a big marquee with a disco and a buffet, which had been organised by the club. Everybody there was just ecstatic and you could see what it meant to them. All the talk was about the Premiership and it was a great night. I couldn't stay as long as some because the next morning I had to be up very early to drive to Lilleshall, where I was going to spend the best part of a week doing the first part of my UEFA A Licence.

In the car, as I headed for the Midlands, I reflected on the events of the previous day and there was no doubt that it had to be the absolute highlight of my playing career. In my time with Middlesbrough there were many highs to accompany the lows, like captaining the team from the old Third Division into the First. Eight of us were from the immediate area and had come through the ranks, so they were special times, although not to be compared with the win at Wembley.

My time with Celtic, between leaving Middlesbrough in November 1991 and joining Ipswich just under four years later, just happened to coincide with one of the least successful spells in the history of the club. I regarded it as a huge honour to represent such a great club but I was suspended and missed playing in the Scottish Cup Final and although I played in the League Cup Final we were beaten and that meant a runners-up medal. I wasn't interested and I doubt if I've looked at it since. I also played for England B but in flitting through the high spots of my career I came to the conclusion that nothing could top that play-off final victory with Ipswich.

As I drove to the Midlands my mind flashed back a few years to when I signed for Ipswich. In my time with Celtic I had suffered the trauma of losing my wife, Bernadette, to cancer. Her death launched a huge campaign to raise money for charity and the Celtic supporters were wonderful. In fact, it seemed everybody wanted to help and for a time I was never away from fund-raising events. I have always thought of myself as a strong person but when I see pictures of how gaunt I had become it is clear that the entire episode had a massive effect on me and I am not ashamed to admit there were times when the strain was too much and I broke down.

Leaving Celtic was also a huge drain on me but I knew the time had come to move on. George (Burley) had been on the phone for weeks, pestering me to make a decision, and in the end I said I would fly down to meet him at Stansted. He took me back to Ipswich, where I had a look around the stadium and behind the scenes, and once I had stepped over the line, so to speak, I was always going to sign.

I look back on my career and in terms of how it finished I couldn't have written the script any better if I'd sat down and penned it myself. The funny thing is that everybody thinks it was planned that I would finish at Wembley, but that is not true. I was pretty close to playing in the opening game of the following season, when we launched our Premiership campaign at Tottenham. In fact, if I hadn't had such a stinker in training on the Thursday or Friday I might well have started that day.

I was registered as a player for that entire season but the simple truth is that the team didn't need me and I was able to concentrate on my coaching duties in what was a great season. On the very last day we went into our final fixture at Derby County still in with a chance of qualifying for the Champions League, but a 1-1 draw at Pride Park, combined with results elsewhere, meant we had to settle for finishing fifth and a UEFA Cup place, which was rightly regarded as an amazing achievement for a newly-promoted club.

In the end it was inevitable that I'd played my last game. Even without my role as a coach, there was no way I was ever going to play on elsewhere. I didn't want to be one of those players who has 10 clubs in the last three years of his career as he winds down. Having said that, you always need to be given the opportunity to move on in your career and I will always be grateful to George, not only for signing me in the first place but for also inviting me to join the coaching staff. I learned a great deal and was able to put ideas into practice that have since benefited me as a manager. Bruce Rioch instilled a real desire for knowledge in me but without the chance to become a coach at Ipswich I have no idea how things might have worked out.

WHEN I LOOK BACK ON that great day at Wembley in May 2000 I have nothing but happy memories of the occasion, although I hope I have also been able to relay the enormous relief that we felt when we knew the job had been completed. Had Barnsley forced an equaliser, I could not say with any real conviction that we definitely would have gone on to triumph in extra time. Things could have, I confess, worked out rather differently, because in football you can never guarantee anything and I cannot stress enough how relieved we all were not to be facing an additional half-hour of play.

But when I think of the players who were around at that time, I know we had a very good squad. I still meet them from time to time in the course of the season, often when I least expect it. For example, I went over to Holland to see an international against Slovenia in October 2007 and who should I bump into but Martijn. Then I went with the West Brom reserves the following week to Lincoln and there was Gary Croft playing left-back for the home side, so we had a chat afterwards.

Of course, I have Mark Venus with me at The Hawthorns and he was such a good player to have alongside me then, just as John McGreal was on the other side. They were true footballers, who could use the ball brilliantly. Our midfielders had no need to drop back and demand the ball off them to get things going, as is so often the case. If they had done, either one of them could have said 'Get away. Why are you going to take it off me? I'm just as good on the ball as you are'.

Either McGreal or Venus could hit a pass that would get us playing, no question about that. Jermaine Wright was an unsung player for us, a really good technical footballer, just as Jim Magilton was outstanding in terms of technique and dictating the game with his range of passing skills, both short and long. Alongside them in the middle we had the skipper, Matt Holland, who gave us drive and determination. He had the energy and was a natural leader as well as a natural winner and, I might say, a wonderful human being.

We had a 3-5-2 formation, which was unusual in itself, but the trick was that we had the players to fit the shape. Was Jamie Clapham, for instance, an out and out left-back? Probably not, but as a left wing-back he had the legs to get up and down all day long, while Crofty was a similar type over on the other side. In a 3-5-2 system the wing-backs are vital and we had two of the best. Up front at Wembley it was Johnno and then Bam-Bam, both equally as effective in their own ways, and alongside them Marcus was a genius at finding space, linking the team up and, of course, scoring goals. We had the right balance and gave every team we came up against problems, something that continued throughout that wonderful 2000/01 season.

JONATHAN WALTERS
STRIKER 2007–PRESENT

BORN   20 September 1983, Birkenhead, Merseyside
SIGNED   26 January 2007, from Chester City, £100,000
IPSWICH CAREER   (to 1 June 2008) 57 games, 17 goals
HONOURS   Ipswich Player of the Year 2008

Jonathan earned his transfer to Ipswich by impressing for previous club Chester City in the two games between the sides in the FA Cup third round in January 2007. He was an almost instant success, although it was when manager Jim Magilton had a brainwave and switched him to the right side of midfield that the one-time Blackburn and Bolton player showed his true worth. Despite moving out of the firing line, Walters revelled in his new role, using his pace and strength, along with his aerial ability, to tremendous effect and becoming one of the most effective members of the side, both in terms of scoring goals and creating chances for colleagues. Such was his impact that scouts from several Premiership clubs regularly had him in their sights, particularly after his first senior hat-trick helped Ipswich to register the biggest Championship win of the 2007-2008 season. Jonathan finished the 2007-2008 season as the club's leading scorer with 13 goals.

Ipswich Town 6 v Bristol City 0

Championship
Saturday 10 November 2007

Portman Road
Attendance 22,020

Ipswich stretch their 100 per cent home league record to 11 games with their biggest win at Portman Road since March 2005 and their most emphatic under manager Jim Magilton

Teams

Jim Magilton	**Managers**	Gary Johnson
Neil Alexander		Adriano Basso
David Wright		Bradley Orr
Alex Bruce		Louis Carey
		(Sub. Jamie McCombe)
Jason De Vos		Liam Fontaine
Dan Harding		Jamie McAllister
Jonathan Walters		Ivan Sproule
(Sub. Gary Roberts)		(Sub. Brian Wilson)
Billy Clarke		Lee Johnson
Tommy Miller		David Noble
		(Sub. Enoch Showumni)
Owen Garvan		Marvin Elliott
(Sub. Sylvain Legwinski)		
Alan Lee		Michael McIndoe
(Sub. Danny Haynes)		
Pablo Counago		Darren Byfield

Walters 5, 55, 72, Wright 15, Goals
Miller 48 pen, Counago 65

Referee: Nigel Miller (County Durham)

THE 2007/08 CHAMPIONSHIP campaign provided a huge number of shock results and this must have been one of them. Not because we won – Portman Road was a fortress at the time – but for the margin of victory. We went into the game sitting ninth in the table, five points behind Bristol City, who were third, and while we were certainly looking to take all three points, just as we had done in our previous 10 home games, I don't think any of us really expected we would hit them for six. But there are days in football when everything just seems to click into place and this was definitely one of them. We could do nothing wrong and City little right, plus they also had a player sent off just after half-time and the more they tried to get back into the game, the more we were able to pick them off and make it an even more emphatic result. Their Brazilian goalkeeper, Adriano Basso, had been named beforehand as the best keeper in the league, according to the ratings, so it was proof all over again that you never really know what to expect once a game kicks off.

The fact that Bristol City declared an interest in signing me from Chester before Ipswich came on the scene was an interesting aside. Mark Wright, the former England defender and manager of Chester at the time, tipped me off that Bristol were keen but he told me that nothing was likely to happen until the summer of 2007, which was when they were apparently geared up to make their move. In the meantime, however, Ipswich came in with a firm offer that Chester accepted and I certainly wasn't going to hang around on the off chance. Actually, when the Chester chairman called me at home one night I was taken aback when he told me of Ipswich's bid. Their interest came right out of the blue. I fully expected him to give me the go-ahead to talk to Scunthorpe, where I had been on loan early in 2005 and who I knew were going to make an offer, but he simply told me a deal had been agreed and the next morning I jumped in the car and drove to Ipswich, where we managed to sort everything out pretty quickly.

I often wonder if the fact that Chester were handed a second chance in the FA Cup was what changed the course of my life. We were actually beaten by Bury but they were thrown out of the competition for fielding an ineligible player and the Football Association reinstated us in their place. I was relishing the opportunity of playing against Alex Bruce, who was in the Blackburn academy with me, and despite the disappointment of having a 'goal' chalked off we were absolutely made up that we managed to earn ourselves a replay. I didn't think I played to the best of my ability in the game but as a team we did okay. Chester's ground isn't the most inviting of places and I believe catching Ipswich on a bit of an off day also helped.

Some of my team-mates were telling me in the dressing room before-hand that Ipswich were keen to sign me but, if I'm honest, I didn't pay any attention to what they said. Thinking about it, maybe they had heard a whisper, but I never did find out the truth. We had some real wind-up merchants at the club and I wasn't going to be taken in. We were looking forward to the second game, which gave us an opportunity to play at a decent ground, and although we went out the two games had been a real bonus after we had lost to Bury but gained an entirely unexpected reprieve.

To sign for Ipswich later that month was incredible. The chairman's call stunned me and after that everything happened very quickly. Suddenly, from being with a League Two club I was signing for one of the top Championship clubs – one that had not only been in the Premiership just a few years earlier, but was determined to return as quickly as possible. In my time at Portman Road, which has so far been tremendously enjoyable, I have often thought about what might have been. If I'd stayed at Chester I might have been injured and then struggled to stay in the Football League, but now I am thinking seriously in terms of going back to the Premiership, where I played briefly with my second club, Bolton, so I will always be grateful to Jim Magilton for having sufficient faith in me to offer me a second chance.

I NOMINATED THE GAME against Bristol City because I scored my first senior hat-trick and it is something I shall never forget. I netted my first goal just five minutes in, cutting in from the right to score with a low, left-foot shot. Generally speaking, I think most left-backs expect their man to go down the outside, but doing the exact opposite has always been a bit of a favourite move of mine. When you do that, one of the central defenders usually comes towards you and that gives you the option of slipping someone else in for a shot. This time, though, I decided to let fly myself and the ball took the slightest of deflections off one of their defenders before ending up in the bottom corner of the net. Believe it or not, it was a move that I had been working on a lot in training and that made it all the sweeter. David Wright headed in a second after 15 minutes and I played my part with a cross that found its way to Alan Lee on the left side of the penalty area. David had done well to continue his run and was picked out perfectly by Alan's centre. City lost skipper Louis Carey to injury midway through the first half, while we also made a change when Danny Haynes came on for Alan, and although we might have scored another two goals we were still very pleased to be 2-0 ahead at the interval.

During the break, the manager hammered home the point that we couldn't afford to relax and assume the job was done, and we started the second half where we had left off at the end of the first by immediately going on the attack to look for a third goal. We didn't have long to wait because City right-back Bradley Orr felt he had no alternative but to bring down Danny as he raced clear inside the box and it was a blatant penalty. Not only that, Bradley was sent off and it clearly wasn't going to be City's day. Bradley's a Liverpool lad who I'd come across in youth football up there and he was mouthing off a bit before that incident. Because there was no Alan Lee, it was left to Tommy Miller to take the penalty and, as Ipswich fans know only too well, he never misses from the spot. Basso might have gone the right way but he wasn't anywhere near quick enough to have any chance of saving it

Our fourth goal was pretty special in that we worked the ball very quickly from one end of the pitch to the other, although it wasn't actually what it seemed. Billy Clarke won the ball in the left-back area and played an excellent pass of about 40 yards to Owen Garvan. At the time it probably looked as if Owen had played me in on the right, where I seemed to have acres of space, but having seen the replay over and over again I can confirm that he was tackled by one of their players just as he was about to make the pass. It was from the challenge that the ball found its way to me and from that moment I had only one thing on my mind – to keep my head down and hit the target. The sheer power of my shot beat their keeper on his near post as I drove the ball high into the net. We had a few players in the box by the time I shot and if I hadn't scored I'm pretty sure Pablo Counago would have had something to say to me about not passing the ball to him.

It was from my pass that Pablo scored our fifth and he showed some unbelievable skill to twist his way past several challenges before virtually passing the ball beyond the keeper and into the net. He did brilliantly again with the pass that led to me completing my hat-trick with 18 minutes still to play. We had been defending and once again the ball was in the opposition net within a few seconds. I was on my bike, Pablo spotted my run and played me through with a perfect pass, and I made sure I cut across their defender before I sent a low, right-foot shot past Basso. In the few seconds between collecting the ball and shooting it was pumping through my head that I was on a hat-trick, and it was a fantastic feeling to see the ball hit the net. Who knows, I might have scored again but for the manager deciding my time was up and replacing me with Gary Roberts for the last 15 minutes or so. I was given a tremendous reception as I came off and it was a very special moment for me.

Scoring the hat-trick proved easier than getting my hands on the traditional souvenir, the match ball, which referee Nigel Miller was at first reluctant to give up. I reminded him I had scored a hat-trick and then I wondered if he was serious or not when he replied 'There is a Football League directive that says I must only hand it over once I return to the changing room.' Fair enough, I thought, so once we had gone down the tunnel I asked Wolfe Powell, the club's player liaison officer, if he would fetch it for me. Wolfe quickly returned and said the referee wouldn't let him have it and he would only hand it over if I went in to see him myself. Thankfully, when I went down to his room he was fine, and after a bit of banter between the two of us he let me have the ball. When I heard the referee was a police sergeant in Durham, I wasn't really surprised, because he didn't seem the type you would want to have an argument with. I got the rest of the team to sign the ball and the naughtier messages that some of them wrote on it will have to remain a secret.

Interestingly, I was wearing a pair of brand new boots against Bristol City. I had bought about eight pairs of different sorts at the start of the season and it was only on the morning of the game that I decided on a change. The boots these days are so soft that they don't need breaking in, nor is there any chance of picking up blisters. I just took them out of the box and put them on. Afterwards, I thought it would be a good idea to keep them, so they went back into the box and for our next game I switched to another new pair. I was going to keep the boots that I wore against Bristol City but I decided instead to put them up for auction at the club's end-of-season awards dinner and they raised a tidy sum for charity.

I SUPPOSE THE IRONY of my first senior hat-trick was that it came along after I had been switched from operating as an out-and-out striker to a role on the right of midfield. I did have one game there for Hull at Walsall in April 2005 – a 3-0 defeat in which I was substituted – but it wasn't until more than two years later that I had my second outing in the same position.

I was an Ipswich player by that time, of course, and we were down at Crawley for a pre-season game in July 2007 when the gaffer sent me on for Jaime Peters, who is much more of an orthodox winger, with about 25 minutes left for play. He must have thought I had done well because a week later, when we played Royal Antwerp over in Belgium, he started me there and it wasn't until the 77th minute that he replaced me with George O'Callaghan. I was satisfied with my performance and I stayed in the same position for the home friendly with Panathinaikos. I suppose it was a clue to the manager's thinking that I only played the first half of that game and I was in my new role again when we started the season with a terrific 4-1 home win over Sheffield Wednesday six days later.

By the time we played Bristol City I had scored four goals, I was also making a useful contribution in terms of assists and overall I felt I was getting more accustomed to the role and settling into it well. I'm fortunate in that I have been blessed with a good engine, which enables me to get up and down the flank, and my stamina is one of my main assets. Throughout my career, I've always been hard-working, given 100 per cent and relished the chance to run my direct opponent into the ground – to the point, hopefully, that when his legs are giving up on him I've still got plenty of energy to burn. Another advantage is that having operated as a conventional striker I know the type of service that the front players prefer. I'm not the type who wants to do a series of step-overs before whipping in a cross; there are plenty of skilful wingers out there with all the tricks but whose final ball lets them down. My height is another plus and we got a lot of joy out of Dan Harding hitting diagonal balls for me to head into the middle. Most full-backs lack the aerial ability of central defenders and that is something I look to take advantage of when the opportunity arises. Also, if we are attacking down the left I like to make a late run and with a bit of luck the left-back is ball-watching, which means I have a chance to get a header on target.

I'VE HAD A PRETTY eventful career, I suppose, in that I started in the Premiership, found myself playing in League Two and now I like to think I'm on my back to the top level again. My first club was Blackburn and I had already earned a pro contract at Ewood Park by the time Bolton came in for me. It was a real eye-opener to be in and around the Bolton first team at the start of the 2002-2003 season and my debut came in a brief appearance as a substitute as we lost 2-1 to Charlton in our first home game. If I wasn't on the bench, I was in the squad, and the most important thing was that I felt involved. I was an unused substitute, for example, as we went to

Old Trafford and beat Manchester United 1-0 in front of 67,000 fans and you don't forget an experience like that; only by getting on could it have been any better. Just three days later I went on for the ex-French international Youri Djorkaeff 15 minutes from the end of our home game against Liverpool, which was a massive thing for me as I have been an Everton fan all my life. We were trailing 2-1 at the time but Ivan Campo equalised in the 87th minute, only for Emile Heskey to score a minute later and earn Liverpool a 3-2 win. My full debut for Bolton came in a League Cup-tie at home to Bury in which Sam Allardyce decided to throw in a lot of fringe players and we lost 1-0. I celebrated my 19th birthday around that time and I was pretty pleased with the progress I was making.

Towards the end of that season I went on loan to Hull, where Peter Taylor was the manager. I scored twice on my debut in a 5-1 win at Carlisle and I ended up with five goals in my 11 games for them. At the start of the 2003-2004 season I joined Crewe on loan for a month. I was on the bench for the first game, but because of a painful abscess in a tooth I wasn't able to make even one appearance for them and also missed a Republic of Ireland Under-21 game. In November 2003 I was on the move again, this time for a 12-game loan spell with Barnsley. After another few weeks back at Bolton, where I still had 18 months to run on my contract, I agreed to a permanent move to Hull. Looking back, perhaps I should have stayed at the Reebok, but I was young and wanted to play and that was what made up my mind for me. Hull won promotion from League Two – we were second to champions Doncaster – just three months later.

Hull finished second to Luton the following year to clinch a place in the Championship, but I was headed in the opposite direction to join Wrexham in League Two. The main attraction, to be honest, was that it was about 30 minutes from where Jo and I call home. There was no haggling over money when I met the manager, Denis Smith. They made me an offer and I accepted, simple as that. The reason we were so keen to move back to the North West was that our daughter, Scarlett, had been born with a condition called gastroschisis, which meant that her intestines had developed outside the abdomen. She had an operation that lasted almost five hours but it did not fully cure the problem and after we got her home for a short time she had further surgery when she was about five months old. Her weight at birth was 4lb 10oz and at five months she was less than 9lb, which meant she was still the size of a new-born baby. Nowadays, she is a normal, happy – and, I'm please to say, healthy – three-year-old and we will never be able to thank the hospital staff enough for what they did for her.

It was a difficult time for us all. Jo and I lived at the hospital, sleeping in a bed that pulled down from the wall, because we wanted to be with Scarlett as much as possible. I would go off to training in the morning and then, after a quick shower, I would head straight back to the hospital. The only time we went home was to collect a change of clothing. Peter Taylor and his assistant, Colin Murphy, were extremely supportive, as was chairman Adam Pearson, who is now at Derby. They knew my mind wasn't right and were very understanding. I still played but I tended not to travel much. At the end of the season, when I spoke to the Hull people about moving nearer home, they could not have been more helpful, but it was strange joining Wrexham because they were in administration at the time.

I played most of the games that season for Wrexham, apart from when I was out with a fractured cheekbone, but I have to admit I didn't score too many goals. I remember the assistant manager, Kevin Russell, who is now with another ex-Wrexham player, Darren Ferguson, at Peterborough, telling me that if I could be a bit more prolific I would be playing at a much higher level. At the end of the season I decided to move on when Wrexham's big rivals, Chester, offered me a two-year deal. Again, the location was a bonus, but just seven months later I was on my travels again, this time to Ipswich, where it could hardly be more different.

At Wrexham and Chester I worried about maybe dropping out of the Football League and not being able to play the game for a living any longer, but now I am an Ipswich player I am looking upwards and thinking more in terms of returning to the Premiership, where I only had a brief taste first time round. I really do try to make the most of every hour of every day. I even tend to go into training on my day off because I am so determined to be the best player I can possibly be. I am delighted with the progress I have made at Ipswich and just one year after my transfer from Chester the club came up with a new contract, which runs through to 2011, which I was pleased to sign. I love the club and the area, and in the summer of 2008 my wife gave birth to our second daughter, Sienna Rose.

I just wish my mother was around to see how things have turned out. It is through her – she came from Dublin – that I qualify to play for the Republic of Ireland but she passed away when I was in my last year at primary school. She had bowel cancer and knew about it for a few years, but her and my dad chose not to tell the children until much later on. I have two older brothers and a younger sister, so my dad was kept extremely busy looking after us. He did a fantastic job and we all think the world of him. He carried on with a full-time job and his workload was enormous with all the household chores – cooking, cleaning etc – on top. He was brilliant and even found time to run the kids' team where I first started playing proper organised football. We had a park with four pitches right across the road from our house and because he was the manager he kept the nets in the garage. When my mates and I put them up for a kickabout we thought we were at Wembley. I still see about eight of them when I go home and we all agree it was the best of times.

It was only years later, after we grew up, that my brothers, sister and I fully understood how much Dad had done for us. He has since remarried and set up his own business – he is a geologist – but he still finds time to come down to Ipswich and see a game every now and then. He missed the Bristol City game but he was there to see me score the only goal against Crystal Palace. He's also a very keen Evertonian and when I get the chance I try to arrange to go to Goodison with him, although opportunities are quite rare. Dad was still playing Sunday League football when he was 51 and is still up for the five-a-sides whenever possible.

As a kid I played at an age group one year ahead of my own and when I was 13 I moved to another club. We were unbeaten for three years and won a national knockout under-16 competition. The closest games were the ones we won 3-0 or 4-0 but we even had a 36-0 victory and I remember scoring 11 in one game. Our home pitch was just 50 yards away from Prenton Park and two of our lads signed for Tranmere. I was playing for the county side but I had got to the stage where I was considering whether to stay on for sixth form, or leave and start work, when Blackburn offered me a four-year contract. That was the start of my roller-coaster career but now I'm at Ipswich I tend to think the only way is up.